John Coleman Adams

Christian Types of Heroism

A study of the heroic spirit under Christianity

John Coleman Adams

Christian Types of Heroism
A study of the heroic spirit under Christianity

ISBN/EAN: 9783337213411

Printed in Europe, USA, Canada, Australia, Japan

Cover: Foto ©Lupo / pixelio.de

More available books at **www.hansebooks.com**

CHRISTIAN
TYPES OF HEROISM

A Study

OF

THE HEROIC SPIRIT UNDER
CHRISTIANITY

BY

JOHN COLEMAN ADAMS, D.D.

BOSTON
UNIVERSALIST PUBLISHING HOUSE
1891

University Press:
JOHN WILSON AND SON, CAMBRIDGE.

TO MY WIFE,

IN REMEMBRANCE OF THE HELP AND SYMPATHY
SHE GAVE TO THE STUDIES FROM WHICH
THIS LITTLE BOOK HAS GROWN,

I NOW DEDICATE IT.

CONTENTS.

	PAGE
INTRODUCTION	7

I.
THE MARTYRS	13

II.
THE APOLOGISTS	37

III.
THE HERMITS AND THE MONKS	61

IV.
THE PRELATES AND THE KNIGHTS	87

V.
THE REFORMERS	113

VI.
THE MISSIONARIES	143

VII.
THE PHILANTHROPISTS	165

VIII.
THE STATESMEN	187

CHRISTIAN TYPES OF HEROISM.

INTRODUCTION.

M. ERNEST RENAN, ruminating upon the growing reverence for what are commonly styled the passive virtues, exclaims, "How feeble would be a society of perfect beings!" His lament over the millennium is a condensation of what is unquestionably a wide-spread feeling about the militant types of ethical character. The charge is frequently brought against Christianity that it bestows a special patronage upon the passive virtues, reversing the honors men have usually paid to those of the heroic type, and claiming for meekness the praise which once went to courage, and for self-sacrifice what used to be bestowed on personal force. Christian ethics, it is said, do not encourage the active and aggressive qualities. The Christian ideal lacks force. Its spirit deprecates the wrestling energy which has won all the world's battles. Its saints are feeble; its code is unfriendly to the strong; its millennium is a reign of effeminacy. Once let the spirit of Christianity prevail, this criticism urges, and you will witness under its refinements the disappearance of the active virtues, the decline of physical courage, the prowess which shone in battle, the intrepidity of manhood, the force which has overcome chaos and built a civilization. We shall see the type degenerate and perhaps disappear, and we shall only be allowed to honor the virtues of the warrior, the patriot, and the knight as the best products of a benighted past.

But justice to Christianity demands a revision of this common judgment. It is deficient at two points. It is not true to the facts of Christian ethics nor to the facts of Christian history. It misconceives the real nature of the dispositions which Christianity inculcates and it is inconsistent with the actual manifestation of the Christian spirit in its historic development. A brief analysis of those virtues to which paganism gave an undue distinction will discover in their constitution a large admixture of what are known as the milder traits. A survey of Christian history will prove that there has been no falling off in the culture of a vital personal force since the ethics of Calvary superseded those of the Platonist and the Stoic.

Turning for a moment to the first of these propositions, I affirm that this objection does not allow for the extent to which the passive virtues enter into the dispositions we call heroic. The passive virtues are not merely negative traits. The commonest types of active strength show a large admixture of the submissive forms of excellence. It costs as much to bear the pressure of adversity and the inertia of sluggish evils as it does to encounter and to overthrow them by assault. Victory waits for the heart in which courage to attack mates with patience to wait and fortitude to endure. "Who does not suffer," says the proverb, "does not win." The strength which bears down opposition, which upsets and resists and encroaches and carries by storm, must be supplemented by the strength which can control self, endure, submit, concede, and bide the turning of the tide. In the very field in which the martial and the patriotic virtues shine most brilliantly, underlying personal prowess, bold generalship, defiance of danger, is a strength knit up of implicit obedience, the abnegation of self, the submission of the subordinate to the superior will. The glory of the conqueror's crown shines with the mild lustre of the passive virtues.

The spirit which won the civil war in America was as much obedience as valor, patience in the long campaign as courage in the charge. The characteristics of our country-men burned not more in the ardor which swept up the steeps of Lookout Mountain and crowned the hills of Gettysburg with invincible steel, than in the fortitude which kept the heart of patriotism unwasted through the privations of southern stockades. The tale of the nation's march to triumph in the later days of the war forms no more brilliant chapter in her history than the persistence, the steadfastness, the patience through dark days of defeat in the field and discouragement in the council-chamber. The moral stamina which decided that conflict was the fusion of vigorous manhood, which

Introduction.

took the field and flung life itself into the dripping scales of battle, and the endurance of womanhood, triumphing over fears and bearing the awful suspense in the silence of the home.

The same things may be said of the men who in braving the perils of strange countries have won the credit of daring, of energy, of vigorous enterprise. They too mingle with their restless power the sterling elements which Christianity but promotes to their proper dignity. If an unknown continent is to be explored or men are sought to break the barricades of the polar zones, more is demanded than the ardor of ambition or the daring which loves great risks. Braided in with these must be the necessary traits of patience, self-denial, fortitude. The pathetic story of Columbus celebrates a patience worthy of the martyrs. But for the passive virtues which reinforced the resources of that intrepid soul, America might have awaited her discoverer another century and the rising life of the modern world been held in check a hundred years. And who does not see how near lie the Christian to the heroic virtues when he remembers that it was Livingstone the missionary who became the explorer of the "dark Continent," and that it is Stanley the explorer who has blazed a path now trodden by the missionaries through the forests of West Africa?

This, briefly, is the answer which may fairly be made upon the general principles of ethical characteristics to the charge that Christianity is debasing the stuff of which heroes are made. And if the charge be inconsistent with a true analysis of the character it fosters, we shall find a cumulative line of testimony in favor of the tonic character of Christian principles, traced in the memorials of the Christian centuries. To these records we appeal with confidence that we shall find that notwithstanding the growing refinements of the active virtues under the tutelage of Christianity, they suffer no diminution of force and brilliancy.

I.

THE MARTYRS.

AND when he had opened the fifth seal, I saw under the altar the souls of them that were slain for the Word of God, and for the testimony which they held. — *Rev. vi. 9.*

> Little they dream, those haughty souls
> Whom empires own with bended knee,
> What lowly fate their own controls.
>
> KEBLE: All-Saints' Day.

Thus, also, said the other martyrs: Do what you will, for we are Christians and do not sacrifice to idols. — *The Martyrdom of the Holy Martyrs*, ch. iv.

> They trod beneath them every threat of man,
> And came victorious all torments through;
> The iron hooks that piecemeal tore their flesh
> Could not their valorous souls subdue.
>
> Breviary.

I.

THE MARTYRS.

THE story of the early martyrs of Christianity takes us back to the first great battle-ground on which Christian heroism was put to the test; and it would be difficult to find in the annals of the times in which these sacrifices were made in witness to the truth, any trial more severe to courage, endurance, and manly nerve. Those who espoused the cause of the cross were called upon to enlist in a service far more exacting than that imposed on any Roman soldier in all the Empire's legions. For they were engaged in a fight which ran from day to day and from year to year. It was a battle three hundred years long; and it was won at last through the unflinching courage and steadfastness of those who by conduct and by creed, in deed and in debate, convinced the heathen world that Jesus of Nazareth was the Sent of God.

There is a legend of early Christianity, to be heard in every country from the Ganges to the Mississippi, which runs as follows. In the middle of the fifth century the owner of an estate near Ephesus accidentally discovered a sealed cavern on his land, in which to his astonishment were seven young men of aspect so strange that the slaves who opened the cave were terrified and fled. When the light fell upon the sleepers they arose and sent one of their number for food. As he journeyed toward the neighboring city he was struck by many unfamiliar sights, and when he came to stand in the streets of his native town it seemed like a metropolis of foreigners. He entered a baker's shop and in payment for his bread offered a coin of the Emperor Decius, two hundred years out of circulation. The astonished shopkeeper arrested him as an owner of unlawful treasure, and being arraigned before the court he told his affecting story. He and his six companions had taken refuge in that cave, as he supposed, the night before from the horrors of the Decian persecution and were pursued and walled in by their foes. When the sun next fell upon them they rose and came forth. And in reply to this story he was astounded to hear that Decius had been dead two hundred years; that for a full century paganism had been supplanted by the persecuted religion; that the capital of the empire had been removed from Rome to Constantinople; and that these seven sleepers of Ephesus had come to life under the second Theodosius, a Christian emperor. Such is the legend of the Seven Sleepers of Ephesus; and it emphasizes with a remarkable picturesqueness the rapid changes which swept the ancient world, from the time that Stephen died in Judea till the day that Constantine reigned in the city of his founding. That which must have seemed a dream to the waking youth of Ephesus was a solid and bitter reality to the men and women whose devotion and courage wrought the mighty change. So while we traverse in thought that period and a little more, which covers the long sleep of the young men of the legend, let us feel as we ought the tremendous personal forces, as well as the mighty principles which turned foes to friends and glorified the cross of Calvary into the heavenly symbol of Constantine's vision.

The first encounter of Christianity was with the bigotry and intolerance of Judaism. It was a conflict with home associates and associations. It was a verification of the prophecy of Jesus himself, who said, "I am come to set a man at variance against his father," "And a man's foes shall be they of his own household." But no opposition calls for sterner stuff in him who means to withstand it than that which comes from one's friends and neighbors, the heretic's family, his intimates, his patrons, or his clients. Bigotry is never more brutal and hostility never more hateful than when they are turned against those who have been companions and co-workers. The Christian could not evade the sweep of a general law, and so he suffered as his Master had done before him. The same spirit which had pursued Jesus to His death followed His disciples. Christianity was received from the very outset with a storm of bitter opposition; and although there was almost always a little party among the Jews who perceived the light and heard the word gladly, the great mass of Jesus' countrymen resisted the progress of the gospel with all the intensity of which a Jew is capable.

The first overt act was the attack made on Stephen. It is a thrilling picture which shows us this brave young man telling his friends and neighbors their mistake, setting their sins in order before them, braving all their wrath, and at last struggling to his knees under the pelting shower of stones, with a prayer on his lips which was an echo of that on Calvary, " Lord, lay not this sin to their charge," and falling asleep with the glory of heaven on his countenance. Thus died the first Christian martyr, and thus to this day we behold him, —

> " All radiant with celestial grace
> Martyr all o'er and fit to trace
> The lines of Jesus' death."

The next to die was James the son of Zebedee, who perished by the sword. James the younger, called the Lord's brother, was thrown from the Temple and beaten to death with a tanner's club. Peter is said to have died in the amphitheatre and Paul to have been beheaded in the Appian Way. Of the other apostles we know nothing certainly. Legends there are to be sure, but nothing more. The Christian was everywhere a man to be hated and opposed, but as yet the sect had not gained prominence enough to be persecuted. There is such a thing as a contempt which does not think it worth while to persecute, and apart from the malice and hate with which a Jew necessarily treated these heretics from the faith of Abraham, there was as yet no widespread movement against the followers of the Lord. In that great, busy, self-absorbed empire, Christianity was not for some years of enough importance to be persecuted.

But that could be true only for a little while. The Christians were aggressive. They were full of a missionary spirit. They journeyed far and wide, always fearless in speech, bold in belief, tenacious of their purpose to tell to others the great tidings they themselves had heard. The spirit of that age in the Church was incarnate in the person of Paul on his endless wayfaring to and fro in the world, speaking the word of truth. With such persistent preaching the Word and its fol-

The Martyrs.

lowers spread. The word "Christian" began to be a "by-word" in strange and distant cities. All that the historian Tacitus knew of them was that they were "a set of men detested for their enormities, whom the common people called Christians." By the year 64 A.D. they had made their way to Rome, and were then prominent enough in the throngs who crowded thither to attract the malevolent notice of Nero himself. In July of that year there was a terrible conflagration in Rome. For six days and seven nights it swept through the city, unchecked and ruinous, till of the fourteen districts or wards only four remained untouched. Three were completely in ashes, palaces, temples, market-places, basilicas, houses, — all were destroyed. There was terrible misery in Rome. There was more than a suspicion that Nero himself had furthered or connived at the destruction. He was accused of wanting to burn Rome that he might rebuild it in more splendid style. He was believed to have had the awful craving for just such a sensation as a city in flames could give him. There was a deep-seated and deadly suspicion of him in the public mind, and the wily emperor must divert it; and so he singled out the Christians. He caused them to be called the incendiaries. There was no reason given for the horrible charge, no crime was brought to their doors, no trial ever was allowed them. But with a senseless fury, all the ingenious cruelty of that diabolical mind was let loose against the Christians. Whoever confessed to being of their number was apprehended and condemned. And when the awful scene of their torment and their death is recalled, it silences all cavil against the courage which persisted in the faith in the face of such horrible deterrents.

For on a dreadful summer night in the gardens of Nero, which once occupied the ground where now St. Peter's rises, there were throngs of the Roman people; and in and out among them moved Nero, in the dress of a charioteer. They had come thither to see an illumination. Along the paths of the garden were huge torches, held aloft on high posts, and flaring and flaming with seething pitch. If the crowd surged up about each one of these with a strange curiosity, it was no wonder. For they were living torches, each one a Christian, each one a martyr in his gown of fire! Moreover not a stone's throw away, - almost in the light of these ghastly beacons, men and women of this name and calling, sewn up in the skins of beasts, were being thrown to famished dogs. So awful was this early test put upon the courage and the endurance of the Christian character.

This was but the beginning of evils. Domitian, because he heard that the Christians were organizing a kingdom, planned a persecution, though it was not carried out. Trajan enacted a law that while Christians must not be sought out, yet when accused and convicted they must be put to death. There were outbreaks of severity and hate under Marcus Aurelius, becoming more severe under Decius and under Diocletian, who held a bitter determination to crush this kingdom within a kingdom. For three hundred years, with every excess and refinement of savagery of which the hard and ingenious mind of cruel emperors was capable, the Christians were pursued and wearied with persecution. It is impossible now to dwell upon the lurid picture of their sufferings; the torments they were called to go through; the strain put upon their endurance and strength of conviction. By far the most dreadful thing about these tortures was that, as Dr. Uhlhorn says, they "did not aim at the death of the Christians, but only at compelling them by means of torture to recant." "Tortures overtook them," says Cyprian, "wherein the torturer ceases not, without escape of condemnation, without the consolation of death." All the ordinary modes of inflicting pain were exhausted long before the malevolence of the persecutors was appeased. When the fire had burned its hottest, and the sword cut its sharpest, and wild beasts had raged their fiercest, and these steadfast men and women were undismayed, then they were stretched and broken upon the rack, and some had their limbs dislocated and their fingers crushed, and others had their flesh torn with sharp hooks, and others were smeared with honey and exposed to stinging insects. Women were insulted and abused in fashions too horrible to be told. It is an awful catalogue, and there is no use whatever in rehearsing it. One single instance will show as well as five hundred the spirit in which the Christians met this attack upon their faith through their persons and their lives. During the reign of Marcus Aurelius, a maiden of Lyons named Blandina was apprehended as a Christian along with many others. She made no denial. Her one answer to every demand was simply, "I am a Christian, and there is no wrong done among us." She was tortured till the breath was almost gone from her body, and then she was revived that she might be thrown into prison. There she was forced to witness the torture and the death of many others, whom she comforted and helped with her strong, cheering words of faith. At last, when her tormentors despaired of making her recant, she was taken from her lingering torture-house for one more sharp distress, and wrapped and bound in a net, was tossed to death upon the horns of a wild bull.

Always distinguished among honored martyrs of this age was Polycarp, the pupil of Saint John. He was arrested by the officers of the governor, and dragged away to the hall of justice. There the governor met him, and with a little compassion for the old saint, urged him to conform to what was asked of him, "only to cry 'Cæsar' twice and sacrifice, and he would be safe." But to all the entreaties and commands Polycarp made reply, "Eighty and six years have I served Christ and He has never done me wrong; how then can I blaspheme Him now,—my King and my Saviour." The officers threatened him with the wild beasts, but he was unmoved. They added the threat of fire. He answered, "Do with me what you will." The crowd clamored for his death. They demanded that he should be burned alive, and rushed for fagots and for wood that he might be made an instant victim. They would have nailed him to the stake, but he said, "Leave me as I am. He who gives me grace to bear the flame will help me to stand unshaken." And so he died, with a prayer of praise on his lips, as stoutly and bravely as any soldier in battle.

In like spirit, when Justin was brought to the trial which won him the surname of "The Martyr," he sealed a life of brave service with as valorous a death. "Sacrifice to the gods," was the rough order of the Prefect. "I am a Christian and cannot

The Martyrs.

sacrifice to idols," was the answer. Then he was led forth, praising God, to the place of execution, where he was first scourged and then beheaded with the axe. It is no wonder that the endurance of the Christians wearied their persecutors. There is no headway to be made against such courage and steadfastness. This was the very heroism which had stood up in the pass at Thermopylæ, and marshalled itself in the plain of Marathon, and hurled back the Carthaginian from the gates of Rome, rallying once more in the hearts of an undegenerate posterity.

There is a picture by Gabriel Max which will convey to any sensitive imagination all the terror and the testing of those early persecutions. It is called " The Token." A young girl with a pure and beautiful face is standing in the arena, in the midst of furious beasts tearing one another in their wild struggles for their human victims. Two of them are grappling at her feet, and beside her a tiger is just rushing from his cage, which in a moment will glut his hunger on her flesh. But she has no thought of them; some one in the throng which waits to see her "butchered to make a Roman holiday"— perhaps a friend, perhaps a lover — has dropped a flower over the parapet, and it lies at her feet, a token of at least one loving heart among all the throng of foes. And as she stoops to pick it up, she has raised her eyes as if to search for the face of her friend. There is no fear in them, no coward wavering in her countenance, but all is serene there with the steadfastness of perfect trust and purity. In a moment the beasts will be upon her. Their angry roar will be drowned in that fiercer one from the throats of twenty thousand men and women who love to see the Christians die, and she will be added to those courageous souls of whom it is said, "The blood of the martyrs is the seed of the Church."

Now I do not allege these experiences of the martyrs as proofs that they were doing unheard-of things or showing unparalleled traits. It is not our proposition that the Christian hero is a new and singular type in so far as his sacrifices and achievements are concerned. It may be conceded that other men had suffered torment with heroism, that other women had braved peril and death with fortitude. That is not to the point. We are aiming now to show that in these new martyrs we have as genuine heroes, displaying a strength as firm, a power as decisive, an aggressive force as vital, as had ever been exhibited; and we merely point to these men and women, dying by hundreds and by thousands the violent deaths which had been counted always as the last tests of virile courage, the experiences which proved whether according to the old standard men were manly, and declare that in this first display of the qualities which it tends to foster, Christianity produced a style of manhood which shows no weakening in the old stock. We look at the men drawn up in the ranks of the Roman legion, we turn to the daring adventurers who are scouring the northern seas in their warships, we even drop a glance of admiration on the gladiator in his brawny strength, and we think it were a pity to lose this courage to face danger unflinchingly, this nerve which can endure physical pain without weakening. Very well. Here in custody of the soldier, here facing the gladiator, here on the coasts where the

Viking buccaneers are winning their fame, are men and women who under the impulse of a purely religious motive are bearing as much and daring as much. The Christian martyr is as vigorous and aggressive a man as any of his contemporaries.

For remember how they are brought to these sufferings. They are not merely standing on the defensive. They have attacked the older faiths; they have rebuked the heathen life by the purity of their own. We underrate these saints of the Church if we reckon them as either passive or pusillanimous. Their very meekness is a sign of the highest strength. It means not passivity, but power. A weak man cannot be a meek man. There is no meekness about one who endures wrong because he has not the vigor to protest against it. That is cowardice, pure and simple. But meekness is that strength which out of strong passions brings a stronger self-control and by means of that force maintains the ascendency of the higher nature and the moral order over the lower. The beauty of meekness lies in the fact that it is the docility, the quiescence of a soul submissive to no will but the Divine, and emptied of the distracting and weakening elements of selfishness. But it is the humility of strength and not the servility of feebleness.

Call the martyrs meek, then, if you will. It is the highest tribute you can pay them. But remember what force of character that term implies and how entirely consistent it is with the most active and aggressive traits. And contrasting the work and the warfare of these men and women with the heroism of the older types, you will seek vainly for any falling off in the quality of the trait. Who could be braver, stronger, hardier, than he whose every-day life puts him in daily danger of death? What soldier called to the shock of arms; what sailor plunging into the midnight gale; what hunter confronting the lion in his lair; what explorer among the ice floes or the jungles; what Columbus braving the perils of an unknown ocean was ever called to the display of a finer courage, a more brilliant intrepidity, a more dauntless endurance? These earliest heroes of the Church were soldiers fighting a daily battle. They were mariners caught in the storm of three hundred pitiless years.

They braved a power more deadly than arctic cold, more withering than tropic heats. With no weapon in hand they composedly faced the hungry beasts on the sands of the arena. Ay, more than that, like explorers in the spiritual world, they put to sea upon uncharted tides, to seek in the kingdom of their Lord a continent unseen of mortal eyes!

But let us add to this word the one additional thought needful to do exact justice to the Christian martyrs. In their conduct they showed, indeed, no falling away from the most superb heroic qualities. In their motives they surpassed all earlier types as the saint surpasses the savage. The spirit and purpose in which they lived and died at once elevates them into a new class. Take two soldiers and let them be fighting with the same physical courage, — the one as a hired mercenary at the bidding of a despot, the other the freeman's battle for his country, — and which becomes the nobler figure; whose courage now is of the sort that wins most admiration? The character of the combatant shines out upon his conflict, and what he *does* gains a glory or a shadow from what he *is*. The man who fights for a price sinks into insignificance by the side of the man who fights for an idea, a principle, an affection. The man who bears pain or braves danger from selfishness or any mean motive grows not greater but smaller from his suffering. But let the motive rise and let him become the servant of something outside himself and higher than himself, and his bravery then is glorified into a real heroism. And to own the sway of a noble idea; to feel, as these men and women did, the mastery of divine truth; to turn loyally whither it beckons, and follow even unto pangs and death,— that is always a more glorious because a more manly and womanly thing than to fight wild beasts or defy the bite of pain.

There is a familiar picture by Gêrome which illustrates with a peculiar force the spirit that was in the souls of the martyrs, its transcendent superiority to the brute courage of barbarous men, and above all its conquering power over human hearts. It represents a gladiator standing in the arena over his prostrate antagonist, and waiting the signal which is to give the poor wretch his life or condemn him to a bloody death. At first glance it seems only a repulsive picture of a brutal deed, devoid of moral interest save as a study of a barbarous sport. But if you look again you will feel a thrill of admiration, not unlikely moistening into tears. For the outstretched fingers of the prostrate youth are not reaching up for pity nor in any gesture of despair. He is making the sign of the cross. He is a Christian. He is dying for principle. He will not recant his faith even there on the bloody sands, with the savage Roman mob yelling his death-sentence in his ears and with the whirling blade of his adversary swooping toward his heart. Who is the braver man, — the hired mercenary or the devoted youth? Whose courage most impresses, sways, moves the heart of the world? For your answer look at the crumbling Coliseum at one end of Rome, type of the coarser aggressive traits; and at the other the cross that crowns St. Peter's with the emblem of the finer courage that dies for truth, the heroism that spends itself for love!

If the work is to be judged by its results and the character by what it effects, then must the heroism of the martyrs be counted of the highest sort. For it was decisive in its success. In this first struggle of the Church with its foes it closed with the brute force of the Empire. Whatever physical powers could do against the Christians was done without stint. And it all failed. It was force against love, and "love never faileth."

> Cross against corselet,
> Love against hatred,
> Peace-cry for war-cry.
> Patience is powerful;
> He that o'ercometh
> Hath power o'er the nations.

II.
THE APOLOGISTS.

I HAVE fought a good fight, I have finished my course, I have kept the faith. — 2 *Tim.* iv. 7.

> Then to side with truth is noble,
>   When we share her wretched crust
> Ere her cause bring fame and profit
>   And 't is prosperous to be just;
> Then it is the brave man chooses,
>   While the coward stands aside,
> Doubting in his abject spirit,
>   Till his Lord is crucified,
> And the multitude make virtue
>   Of the faith they had denied.

This is the victory that overcometh the world, even our faith. — 1 *John* v. 4.

There is a strength of quiet endurance as significant of courage as the most daring feats of prowess. — TUCKERMAN.

II.

THE APOLOGISTS.

NO age is appreciated if it be seen only from one point of view; for every standpoint brings out one set of characteristics at the expense of others. The story of the martyrs, for instance, brings vividly to mind the physical heroism of the early Christians. It reveals the splendid intrepidity with which these first disciples in the new school of ethics and religion faced the same old adversaries, — pain, peril, and death, — which have been the tests of heroism from the beginning of time. But the simple story of their sufferings does not do justice either to their sacrifices or to the full strength of their heroic temper.

For there is a heroism in creed as well as in deed. There is a heroism in thinking as well as in acting, — in which, indeed, thought *is* action and is the form which personal force assumes. And the growth of the soul of man develops a kind of courage and of heroic strength not to be found in the earlier and lower types of men. For as time goes on and man unfolds his inner nature, it soon appears that the same courage and endurance which will sustain him in physical perils fails him in trials of a higher and more searching sort. Says Dr. Chapin: "At the bottom of a good deal of the bravery that appears in the world there lurks a miserable cowardice. Men will face powder and steel because they cannot face public opinion." The same man who will brave the tempest or move at the head of the charging column dares not hold an opinion at variance with the creed of his neighborhood. A man may dare the high seas without a shadow of fear, who never will venture off the safe soundings of popularity or tradition in thought. There were men who gave their lives for this country when they felt the united sentiment of their loyal countrymen behind them, who nevertheless did not dare to side with Garrison and Phillips in that unpopular sentiment which isolated the great agitators. It was easy to bear privations and wounds in comparison with the trial of standing by an unpopular opinion in a time of social persecution. In truth, the man or woman who espouses a new truth, subscribes to a creed which is reckoned heretical, or steps out into any position of difference with the opinions or the morals of his neighbors in life, is called upon to display a rare and high courage, a heroism harder to find and more difficult to sustain than that which goes with the multitude to battle.

It is to the contemplation of such a type of courage that we turn when we review the opening centuries of the Christian era, with our eyes this time upon the intellectual and the moral struggle that was fought to a victorious end under the lead of the apologists, the defenders of the faith. Let us realize that long before these men and women were led to the stake or thrust into the arena, they had displayed that kind of courage which leads the way to great reforms and makes possible the world's moral renovation. For they had dared to separate themselves from the sympathy of their age; they had arrayed themselves in hostility to the ruling faith and the common conduct of life; they had set at defiance custom, fashion, interest, law, and prejudice; they had arrayed themselves in radical opposition to all the tangible forces of their age. "Christianity," says Professor Smythe, "from the beginning had to encounter active and skilful foes. Judaism and heathenism were no abstractions but armed warriors. The struggle was a vital one, — not a question of mere organization or subsidiary doctrine, but of the origin, essence, authority, and power of the gospel. The contest also was protracted. As it went on, all the forces that could be arrayed against the new religion had time to reach the field of conflict and mingle in the strife. The victorious Roman, the acute and versatile Greek, the Oriental theosophist, the Jewish legatist, the power of the Empire, the learning of Alexandria, vested interests, wit, ridicule, sarcasm, reverence for the past, the pride of human reason, the cunning of covetousness, the accumulated resources of human wisdom and human depravity,—all were marshalled and taxed." That is a tremendous array and indicates the storm of hostility and resistance every Christian was sure to encounter when he took his stand with the pure band of the apostles and martyrs. Merely to be a Christian was an act of heroism.

But in order to have a just appreciation of the task which lay before the defenders of the faith, we must bear in mind the familiar facts which describe the condition of the Roman Empire in intellectual and moral life, when the first strange voices were lifted up to herald the name of Jesus the Christ to the world. The tranquillity of the Empire under Cæsar Augustus was a fallacious calm. The realm of the Cæsars was a splendid shell, whose outward glories were more than matched by its inward corruptions. The government was a relentless absolutism. The whole world was at the mercy of one man's will. The people had yielded all their liberties because they were too indolent and too selfish to maintain them; and with the concession of their political prerogatives men had signed away their moral and their intellectual liberties. As power was concentrated immorality increased. The emperors set a frightful example of crime and of vice. Their courtiers were apt pupils, and the contagion spread to the people. Tiberius, Caligula, Claudius, Nero, Galba, and Otho vied with one another in a succession of evil lives. As Dr. Draper, one of the calmest critics, says: "The social fabric was a mass of rottenness. The people had become a populace; the aristocracy was demoniac; the city was a hell. No crime that the annals of human wickedness can show was left unperpetrated." The breach between classes became wider than ever before in history. The rich were very rich; the poor were in most abject misery. Labor had passed into the hands of a vast army of slaves, and so was counted a degradation to a citizen; and great populations in every city demanded to be fed at the public expense. Justice was bought and sold like a commodity. Every man's life was at the mercy of informers and spies. No property was safe from the rapacity of those in power. "Freemen," says Tacitus, "betrayed their patrons, and he who had lived without an enemy died by the treachery of a friend." Poisoning was reduced to a system. Crimes against purity grew more and more nefarious. Marriage was avoided. Illicit passion fed itself with the most enormous excesses. Modesty became a lost virtue. "Women," it was said, "marry that they may be divorced, and are divorced that they may marry." The most distinguished names of the period are stained with unnatural crimes which to-day may not even be named. The awful practice of infanticide increased, and it was reckoned a folly and a frailty to be encumbered with a family of children. Slavery, too, cursed the Empire like a plague-spot. Gibbon estimates the number of slaves at sixty millions. Every conquered province yielded its quota to swell the totals. Whenever a man became a slave, his lot was cast in with the brutes. The utter degradation of manhood may be read in the one fact that slave labor was cheaper than animal labor, and much of the work we perform with cattle was done by men. The slave lived like a brute, was treated like a brute, and died like a brute. He became the pander to his master's lust or the victim of his cruelty. That excellent old man Cato flogged his servants before his guests, and when they were worn out with age in his service sold them like so many old clothes, for what he could get. In Cicero's time, some rich patrician had a slave crucified for killing a wild boar at the wrong moment during a hunt, and all the comment Cicero had to make on such wanton atrocity was the remark, "This may possibly seem harsh."

But the cruelty, wantonness, excess, and sensuality of the Empire rose to its awful climax in the gladiatorial shows. It is hard, almost impossible, for a modern mind to conceive the atrocity of this feature of life under the Empire. That men and women, in what is reckoned an advanced period of civilization, should have made the killing of beasts and men their habitual amusement is almost beyond belief. But there seemed to be no limit to the excesses which were permitted in this constant accompaniment of life in the great cities. The deadly combats between pairs of men, or between a gladiator and a beast, because more attractive than any other sport. The cruel diversion which made all other pleasures insipid soon grew tame itself, and the craving for more dreadful sensations had to be gratified, with every extravagance of violence, bloodshed, and torture. Whole herds of beasts were turned loose in the arena to tear and maim and kill one another. Pompey let loose six hundred lions in one day. The games of Trajan lasted one hundred and twenty days, and ten thousand gladiators fought, and ten thousand beasts were slain. Under Domitian an army of feeble dwarfs was compelled to fight, and more than once female gladiators fought and perished in these ghastly shows.

It must be remembered that these were not the sports of the abandoned and the dissolute; they were the recreation of the multitude. If you had been in Rome on a pleasant summer day you might have gone in with some eighty thousand spectators to the Coliseum, and there found yourself in the presence of every class and condition of Roman society from the Emperor and the vestal virgins down to the lowest beggars and criminals; so that Mr. Lecky calls the great amphitheatre itself " at once the most imposing and the most characteristic relic of pagan Rome."

When the morals of a people have sunk to such a point, it is easy to see how ill it must fare with philosophy and with religion. The time was one of undisguised scepticism and the deepest intellectual depression. Philosophy was but a feeble and wavering guide through these dark times. It led the thoughtful classes to an intellectual atheism, which was matched by the "atheism of indifference" among the common people. Religion was wasted to a degraded superstition. There was a god for every event and every work of life; and the worship of these divinities, whose attributes were so often no more than personified passions and lusts, was little more than a system of bribery for getting their favors. Many a time this so-called worship became an orgy of crime and sensuality. Men had small respect for the gods, who frequently were but exemplars in sin. "If I could catch Aphrodite," said a friend of Socrates, "I would pierce her with a javelin, she has corrupted so many of our modest and excellent women." In one of Terence's plays a man justifies the worst of crimes against the family by saying, "If a god does it, why may not I?" And yet because men feared these deities and sought to avert their ill-will, they were scrupulous to the last degree in the performance of the ceremonies which were supposed to please the gods, and uncontrollable in their rage against any who offered no gifts or supplications. I know no better words than those of Dr. Draper, whose temper would not permit him to do any injustice to paganism, to sum up the conditions which marked the age when the star shone over Bethlehem. "Faith was dead; morality had disappeared. Around the shores of the Mediterranean the conquered nations looked at one another, — partakers of a common misfortune, associates in a common lot. Not one of them had found a god to help her in her day of need. Europe, Asia, and Africa were tranquil, but it was the silence of despair."[1]

I grant that in this very condition there was a profound reason for hopefulness and for faith to any soul with a knowledge of the characteristics of the human heart and the utter impossibility of detaining it long in the degradation of moral corruption and spiritual want. But it needed a strong and courageous mind to believe in the moral resiliency of human nature, and a

---

[1] Intellectual Development of Europe, p. 267.

brave faith in the new religion to see in that the destined means of regeneration. And to any heart which felt the awful demoralization of those days and realized how radical and uncompromising must be the process of the spiritual renovation of this evil condition, the task must have seemed heavy enough to daunt the most fervent and sanguine. Could anything but the most heroic determination and the most unswerving faith have given impulse enough to lead men forth into the declaration of principles and of an allegiance which practically cut them off from all men? The Roman world was indeed tolerant of many gods, and the worship of a new one would not in itself arouse hostility against his devotees. But when the new god claimed all the devotion of his follower's heart, and pronounced the worship of all other divinities idolatry and superstition, and required a purity of life and a strictness of conduct which was a standing rebuke to the daily walk and conversation of all the world, there is little wonder that prejudice flamed into a fierce opposition and demanded the suppression of this new cult. A Christian man was a social outcast. His citizenship in the kingdom of heaven made him an exile in the Empire; and in that very attitude into which he was forced, he found the sharpest test of his heroic qualities.

For the heroism of the innovator in thought and in faith was an every-day requisition of the defender of the faith. Every act of his made him conspicuous among his fellowmen, thrusting him into that trying prominence so hard for sensitive men to assume. A Christian could not perform the simplest acts nor sustain the simplest relations of life without becoming a marked man. His very scruples accused him. What he abstained from doing was as conspicuous as what he did. Every step was a confession of faith, and every confession brought a new peril. Many a Christian could only have become such by abandoning the business which was his support in life; for if he were a servant or laborer in a pagan temple, if he were a maker or seller of idols, if he were an actor, a soldier, a gladiator, he could be baptized only on the condition that he give up his occupation. His fellowship depended on his abstaining from whatever supported the heathen system or drew a revenue from its corrupted life; and when the spirit of heathenism was everywhere, every hour and every scene exposed the daring alien in faith. He could not go upon the street without passing the images and symbols of the gods, to which custom required him to do homage. If he entered a court of justice or the Senate, there was the altar with wine and incense where he was expected to offer a libation and strew incense. If he gave alms to a beggar, the mendicant might invoke on him the blessing of some god, and if he were not to protest he might seem to accept the blessing of an idol. If he had occasion to borrow money, the note he must sign would contain an oath by the heathen gods. If he were invited to a family gathering of his heathen relatives or friends, his absence would excite remark; and if he went he must incur their displeasure by declining any share in the sacrifices offered from beginning to end of the meal. The Christian wife or husband, son or daughter, was in the most painful plight; for the duties of religion would clash with all the family feelings and make the loyal heart a stranger in its own home.

Now there is no doubt that in the heroism born of such conditions we have a higher type than that which merely makes men endure the pangs of bodily suffering. The latter is a form of human strength which we would never see go out of fashion and which the testimony of the martyrs shows never will go out of fashion under the reign of Christianity; but the latter calls for qualities of a finer order, and under the tutelage of Christianity has met with such a response as under no other system or form of human culture. This constant attrition of the true faith with the false put a strain upon men's souls that exceeded the power of the weak or the morally degenerate. Napoleon used to say that he was fond of "two-o'clock-in-the-morning-courage," or that type which is never surprised, never unprepared for action, never startled into cowardice. But the courage of the men and women who met the forces of heathendom and fought with them the conquering war of the Cross, was a better sort than that. For theirs was a morning, noon, and night courage, capable of taking the longest strain, of endurance, of unflagging earnestness, of tireless patience. It was as good by day as by night, and its forces knew no dusk or midnight. It was equal to the test of sustaining ills which it clearly foresaw, and meeting deliberately the forces from which it expected and asked no conditions and no quarter.

The first labor set for these noble hearts was the defence of the faith. The Christian must defend himself and his religion against the merciless reasoning, ridicule, denunciation, and slander which were turned against him and his religion. It was said that Christians led immoral lives, and they must disprove the charge or courageously live down the slander. The heathen heard the Christians speak of partaking of the body and blood of Christ; and straightway the word went about that these fellows murdered and devoured an infant at their feasts. They heard of the love-feasts of these religionists; and knowing no love but lust, they declared that these secret religious meetings were orgies of licentiousness. Because the Christians had no temples and could not brook the sight of altars and statues, it was declared that they had no gods, were atheists, were responsible for the disasters sent by the jealous and angry deities. Because their aims were little understood, were mysterious and strange to the people, they were charged with forming a secret society, and called disloyal to the Emperor and unprofitable to the State.

To these charges the apologists responded by pointing to the martyrs. "Is it possible," they asked, "that men would die as you see they do who live as you say they do. A life of self-indulgence is not a preparation for a martyr's death." And they appealed to the lives as well as the deaths of the Christians in refutation of this evil slander. It was notorious that many a profligate, many a wanton, many a dishonest person upon embracing this faith had become utterly reformed in character. The heathen were taught the real truths of the Christians' faith and its spirituality enforced upon them with every imaginable argument. They who charged the Christians with disloyalty were challenged to show where they had ever been involved in conspiracy, or failed to serve and honor the Emperor as loyal subjects should, save only in the withholding of those divine honors which they conceived to be impious and contrary to their convictions. Thus they stood sturdily and steadily holding fast by the faith delivered to the saints, — the champions of its truths, the defenders of its good name, the loyal expounders of its novel doctrines.

But they did more than defend. They turned on Paganism. They pushed beyond defence into attack. True, they were only contending for toleration for themselves. But theirs was a mission of conversion; and truth to their convictions, fidelity to the gospel they had espoused, compelled them to go farther and reason with the writers and philosophers of the pagan world upon the absurdity of its beliefs and the pernicious influence of its practices. But here the difficulty was two-fold. It was not hard to expose the folly and absurdity of the popular mythology. The truth of the heathen religion could not be defended. It was absolutely untenable. The philosophers themselves had concluded that it would not bear examination and that no sane man could believe the tales of the gods. At the same time everybody deprecated the attempt to reform or to overthrow the popular faith. It had no moral influence on the people. It had ceased to control thought; but it was a mighty political engine, not to be meddled with, because it was built into the fabric of the State and an integral part of its life. He who touched it must meet all the opposition of vested interests as well as of a superstition as cruel as it was ignorant. And so on the part of the populace, the priesthood, and the princes of the State there was the keenest opposition to every word which could be construed as impiety toward the gods. It might be true that the popular faith was a delusion; but it was a popular one, it was a good thing for the powerful classes, and woe betide him who tampered with it. That was the opposition which met the Christian when he would appeal to the people to forsake the worship of their wicked and impotent deities. "Let be," was the word. "Rome has prospered well under the care of the gods. Beware of any sacrilege." And when popular prejudice is aroused, the man who places himself in its way must be something more than a coward.

The case was no better with the philosophers and their disciples. This was the other difficulty of the Christians. The scepticism of the age required a heart of oak to overcome it. It was destructive, agnostic, hopeless, pitiless, loveless. Philosophy was confused and helpless. It could offer no help and it would receive none. It simply gave itself up to inertness and to despair. To face such a mood requires a heart with more than a passive fidelity. It takes all the vigorous, aggressive belief of which men are capable to go into the field of intellect and there contend against the paralyzing, killing force of a great negation. There is something appalling in an audacious doubt. A great infidelity is a very giant in arms. Many a noble mind has been prostrated before the might of its baleful spirit. Nor are there any men in all the roll of history who merit a higher place of honor and renown than those who armed with a few simple ideas, so simple and so plain that they look like David's sling and pebbles in contrast with the arms and stature of

Goliath, attack the imposing power of false philosophy intrenched in the despair and scepticism of a decaying civilization. To the thoughtful man the spectacle, sometime covering many years, is as thrilling as a great battle. And when at last the truth prevails and the old error goes routed into the shadows, discredited and friendless, something of praise above what is given to the acuteness which planned and the dialectic skill which effected the defeat is due to the brave faith which nerved the hearts of those who first dared utter a protest against the wizard lie that held an age under its spell.

III.

THE HERMITS AND THE MONKS.

OH, that I had in the wilderness a lodging place of wayfaring men that I might leave my people and go from them ! for they be all adulterers, an assembly of treacherous men. — *Jer.* ix. 2.

> The old order changeth, giving place to new,
> And God fulfils himself in many ways,
> Lest one good custom should corrupt the world.
> TENNYSON.

During about three centuries and while Europe had sunk into the most extreme moral, intellectual, and political degradation, a constant stream of missionaries poured forth from the monasteries, who spread the knowledge of the Cross and the seeds of a future civilization through every land from Lombardy to Sweden. — LECKY.

It cost Europe a thousand years of barbarism to escape the fate of China. — MACAULAY.

III.

THE HERMITS AND THE MONKS.

WHEN Rome had become converted to Christianity, she had not been renovated morally. The work of the martyrs and of the apologists had left men changed in belief but not in life. The degeneracy of the Empire was too complete to be overcome in a century. It took hundreds of years for the leaven of the Christian ethics to permeate the social life and institutions of the world. Christianity indeed won a speedy victory over the world's faith. In a marvellously short time the Church had become the teacher of society. But the scholar was slow and inapt, very ignorant, and very undisciplined, and the process of renewing the moral life of the Empire was slow and halting.

In the years to which we now advance, Rome was declining toward her fall. That catastrophe was now impending which Gibbon calls the greatest and perhaps the most awful in the history of mankind. The slow causes which had been at their weakening work for hundreds of years were now developing to their culmination. Every element of Roman life was contributing to the general ruin. The corruption of morals had sapped the manhood and womanhood of the age of all its courage and endurance. The patriotic spirit which built the Empire had long since died by the hand of selfishness and despotism. The disorders of tyranny had thrown down the last barriers which protected the State, and at length the barbarians, pouring down from the north, completed the work of wrecking great Rome. The ruins which to-day stand stark and bare about the Forum show how great that catastrophe was. The great basilica, just across the Tiber, indicates the power which, during those centuries of wreck, pillage, and bloodshed, preserved the elements of social life from complete annihilation. While if you would seek in those same streets of modern Rome the representative of the institution which for centuries embodied the best life and the most vigorous energies of the Church, you would find it in the monk with his cowl and crucifix, who wends his way on errands of piety or mercy. Just as the martyrs and the defenders of the faith embodied in themselves the work of the first three centuries, the hermits and the monks represent the vital energies of the new organization, which was destined to thrive and to wax strong while every other institution of the social life of man was suffering in disease or languishing unto death.

For in the early years of the fourth century there began a new era in the Church; and as every new epoch in history is associated with the name and the personality of some man, so the era of the hermits and the monks is forever associated with the fame of Saint Anthony the hermit. The story of his life is the introduction to the great movement which he led, — the beginning of monasticism, the organization of a force to meet the deteriorations of society. He was a well-born and serious Egyptian youth, orphaned at an early age, and living with his sister; but being impressed by the words of Christ, "Go and sell all thou hast, and give to the poor," he parted with his property, save enough to maintain his sister, and bestowed it upon the poor, while he himself withdrew to the outskirts of a little village, where he dwelt, working, praying, and studying the Scriptures. It was his aim to emulate the best there was in every man he met, and always to strive against the spirit of worldliness, of impurity, of false ambition. He had a fierce struggle with self, and when he deemed that he had overcome in himself the spirit of evil, he nevertheless continued to practise the most rigid austerities, lest he might be overcome in some unguarded moment and fall again to his old estate. For twenty years he dwelt apart, coming forth from his cell only at long intervals, and always practising upon himself all the devices of self-denial, of mortification of the body, of fasting, and of prayer. "He who sits in the desert," he was accustomed to say, "is safe from three enemies, — from hearing, from sight, and from speech. He has only to fight what he finds in his own heart." "He who would be free from sin," said Anthony, "must be so by weeping and by mourning, and he who would be built up in virtue must be built up by tears." His life passed beyond the limits of a century. "At last," one says of him, "he perceived that it was time for him to set sail, for he was a hundred and five years old;" and so one day he said, "I perceive that I am called by the Lord," and lay down to his last sleep.

But his life did not end with this sleep of his body. From far and near disciples had been gathering, who accepted his principles and would imitate his life. His cell became the goal of many a pilgrimage, his discourse a new gospel to many a burdened and world-weary soul. A great host soon followed the lead of Saint Anthony. The deserts and solitary places became the haunts of multitudes who, like the pious Alexandrian, cultivated retirement, fastings, and mortification of the flesh as the means of salvation. Vast populations sprung up, who abode in tombs, in caves, in wells, in every lonely and deserted spot, and these hermits were seized with one intense and sincere passion. They lived apart that they might pray and study and meditate, watch their own hearts and instruct the souls of others, renouncing self and bringing themselves under the most fearful torments and self-inflicted disciplines. Their first principles in the life they had chosen were celibacy and poverty, charity and self-mortification. They became the objects of admiration and of reverence. They were sought out by the best and most virtuous men and women, who found inspiration in their lives and wisdom in their words. Wonderful stories got abroad of the courage they displayed, of the abstinence they practised, of the miracles they wrought. They were accounted the wisest and the best of men. Those who had neither the courage nor the virtue to follow their example, who could neither approve the world nor retreat from it, nevertheless looked in reverence and in gratitude on the men who could maintain their own purity where all around was so vile, and renounce the thought of a personal gain where all others were grasping and selfish. Such eminent and excellent Christians as Athanasius, Basil, Chrysostom, Gregory, Jerome, and Augustine deemed the hermits a noble race and approved their character and their works. The opinion was all but universal which has since been stated by Montalambert, the great historian of this class, that "theirs was the most noble effort that has been made to overcome corrupted nature and to approach Christian perfection."

But the bare narration of this fact does not at all suggest its real significance. It is a wonderful phenomenon indeed under any interpretation. It is no ordinary spectacle which displays to us these hundreds of thousands of men and women forsaking their homes, disposing of their possessions, living without comforts, and inflicting upon themselves the harshest self-mortifications; and one seeks to know the real causes leading up to so general and so earnest a movement. As in the case of most of the great movements of society, this one was the outcome of various forces.

1. In the first place, a movement of asceticism had long been raging, in the words of Mr. Lecky, "like a mental epidemic," throughout the world. Among the Jews, the Essenes, placing themselves

in absolute hostility to the national approval and encouragement of marriage, constituted a monastic society wholly separate from the world. In practical, matter-of-fact Rome the same tendency prevailed, and the sect of the Cynics recommended a complete renunciation of the social and domestic ties. Egyptian philosophy fostered the same general sentiments, and even many of the Christian sects encouraged the practice of penances and the habits of asceticism. It was a mental fashion of the time.

2. But like every other mental mood, this one had a relation to the philosophy which was then dominant. Every practice grows out of some principle. The things men do spring naturally from the thoughts they think; and behind the asceticism of the age, which made so many hermits, was a belief in the essential evil of matter. The doctrine was widely held that matter was inherently bad; that out of man's material nature came all the ills which befall his spirit; and that the only salvation for the soul was through the ceaseless abuse and contempt of the body. There is something

marvellous in a mania which took possession of men's minds and made them abuse and defile God's handiwork in their own bodies. Nevertheless it was a conviction which led up to the practice, and wild and exaggerated as it was, it was sincerely and devoutly held and practised. Saint Jerome tells admiringly of a saint who for thirty years had lived on a small portion of barley bread and a little water, and of another who lived in a hole, and whose daily portion of food was only five figs; and this same holy father had a third hero, who seemed admirable in his eyes because he cut his hair only on Easter Sunday; who never washed his clothes, nor changed his tunic till it dropped in pieces; and whose merits, as shown by these austerities, Homer himself would be unable to recount. It was related of Saint Macarius that for six months he slept in a marsh and exposed his body to the stings of venomous flies. Cleanliness was so far from being regarded as next to godliness that it was treated as a deadly error, and he who washed his body was regarded as polluting his soul. Saint Abraham the hermit, who lived for fifty years after his conversion, rigidly refused from the date of that experience ever to wash his face, and his biographer rather ambiguously remarks that "his face reflected the purity of his soul!" In later years, when this dreadful superstition had somewhat spent its force, a pious abbot, dwelling mournfully on the past, exclaimed in evident reproach of his own times, "Our fathers never washed their faces, but we frequent the public baths!"

The poet Tennyson has caught and expressed the spirit of that age in the lines which describe the life and the self-torment of Saint Simeon Stylites. The story of his excesses in penance is too revolting for refined ears; but he chiefly gloried in the peculiar practice which gave him his title. He built successively three pillars, the last one being sixty feet high, on which for thirty years he remained exposed to every change of climate, ceaselessly bending his body in prayer almost to the level of his feet. For a year, it is said, he stood upon one foot, his body vile with sores and with filth, his mind on the verge of insanity; and this poor starving, shrivelled maniac was only an extreme example of the ideal which all men were disposed to regard as the highest, the most worthy of their endeavor. The words which Tennyson puts into his mouth represent the reigning superstition under whose impulse in part men sought the desert and the hermit's cell, —

> "Bear witness, if I could have found a way
> More slowly painful to subdue this home
> Of sin, my flesh which I despise and hate,
> I had not stinted practice, O my God."

3. But in our search for the causes of the ascetic movement in the dark ages, we are not to forget another truth. If it be a fact that every practice of society grows out of some social conviction, so, too, it is true that every social tendency in thought is born of the practical needs which force themselves on human minds from without. There is a startling correlation between the moral life of man and the philosophical doctrines to which it leads or drives him. Thus when the heart of the world has been long burdened with the teachings of materialism, it throws off the weight in some rebound toward a doctrine which exalts the soul and asserts its

supremacy. Or when society has been long sinking under the excesses of sensuality and debauchery, it is natural that it should recoil to a hatred of the body and a stern mortification of its passions and propensities. The asceticism of the dark ages was a natural result of the corruptions of the later empire. It was the reaction from the wild debauch of sensuality and crime in which the degenerate society of Rome had been indulging. "Men," says Guizot, "were unoccupied, perverted, and a prey to all kinds of miseries. That is the reason we find so many turning monks.... When human nature could not fully and harmoniously display itself, when man could not pursue the true aim of his destiny, it was then that his development became eccentric, and that, rather than escape ruin, he cast himself at all risks into the strangest situations; ... the weariness, the disgust at an enervated perversity, the desire to fly from the public miseries is what made the monks of the east." The attempt to live in purity among men became too great a strain. It was necessary to invoke the aid of solitude, of isolation, in order to begin the moral cure and renovation of themselves and of the world. The flight of the hermits from society was simply their effort to establish a sort of moral and spiritual quarantine, to separate themselves from the contagion of the world's terrible sinfulness, and check by isolation the spread of the awful ravages of sinfulness and corruption. The remedy was harsh, but the disease was malignant.

Just here is the heroic side of asceticism, the phase of an otherwise eccentric, morbid, and unnatural movement, which commands our admiration. It signified a stern and unflinching hatred of sin. It was the expression of men's longing for perfection. These enthusiasts went to the length of self-torture to express their desire for deliverance out of the temptations and the contaminations of an evil world. You may call this ridiculous. From the safe vantage ground of a society which sustains and encourages the practice of virtue, you may pronounce asceticism an absurd mistake, a dreadful error. But if you had lived in the day in which asceticism throve, you would probably have taken a different view of it. To a well man the diet of the sick room doubtless must always seem weak and detestable, but doubtless it is the best diet for a sick man. And so apparently the best way the dark ages afforded out of their miseries and depravities was the way the hermits took. It was the only road to a religious and spiritual life. It is to be hoped that such an age may never recur, but if ever it does we shall behold a similar reaction. If the world ever again falls into the degeneracy of the later empire, there will be a new reign of asceticism before it is reclaimed; and in that day we shall all see and admit the strength and the courage which led men even to such fanatical extremes. There is a moral heroism in the fulfilment of the principle of self-renunciation, of separation from the world, of the immolation of self; and the age to which such examples are set, the age which learns that human nature can live upon a plane far above its own greed and violence, and fraud and lust, in an atmosphere of self-sacrifice and peace and fraternity, will as inevitably revere the strength and the virtue of those who teach it to live above this flesh, as the men and women of the fourth century revered the names of the hermits, from Saint Anthony on.

But the movement toward solitude and asceticism did not end in itself. Its principles were at the foundation of a broader and more systematic movement. Its practice was the basis of a form of religious life which is perpetuated to the present day. The hermit was lineally and logically the predecessor of the monk. The monastery is the fruit of the hermitage. The steps by which the evolution was made are simple enough. The followers of the holy men who first led the way into the deserts built their own huts side by side, and while they continued to live each in his own abode, joined in their religious exercises and so began to establish a common life. It was at this time, according to Guizot, that they were first called monks. But by and by they took another step. Instead of remaining in separate huts they collected in one edifice, under one roof; and thus was reached the form of life and administration which ruled Europe for centuries; and thus were formed the great houses of piety, of learning, and of missionary zeal, which preserved literature through the dark ages, which nourished the religious life of a dreary and desperate time, and which furnished the master spirits who overcame the conquerors of Rome and tamed the wild spirits of the barbarians of the north. These new and strange communities multiplied in number and in population. In the stately words of Gibbon: "The prolific colonies of monks multiplied with rapid increase on the sands of Libya, upon the rocks of Thebais, and in the cities of the Nile. To the south of Alexandria the mountain and adjacent desert of Nitria was peopled by five thousand anachorets, and the traveller may still investigate the ruins of fifty monasteries which were planted in that barren soil by the disciples of Anthony. In the upper Thebais the vacant island of Fabenne was occupied by Pachomius and fourteen hundred of his brethren. That holy abbot successively founded nine monasteries of men and one of women; and the festival of Easter sometimes collected fifty thousand religious persons, who followed his angelic rule of conduct."

Egypt was indeed the parent of the

monasteries; but there was soon scarcely any Christian country in which a similar movement was not ardently propagated. It was encouraged by the most eminent men in the Church. It was espoused by some of her strongest and best spirits, and in a very short period the foundations were laid for the great monastic orders, — those institutions which entered so powerfully into the life of Europe for the next thousand years.

The organization of the great orders of monasticism began with the founding of the Benedictines by Saint Benedict about the beginning of the sixth century. Benedict was an Italian of the duchy of Spoleto and educated at Rome. But wearying of the profligacy and the corruption he saw all about him and becoming inbued with the spirit of the monks, at the age of fifteen he himself became a hermit. The fame of his great sanctity spread abroad and brought great crowds about him, who begged his prayers and sought his counsels, so that at last he was led to found twelve monasteries, in each of which he stationed twelve monks. This was at Monte Cassino, and out of this community, to which he gave rules and a system of discipline, came the great order which for thirteen hundred years has endured and perpetuated his name. The rules of the Benedictines were severe and trying. It was no child's play to be a monk in the days when this great order flourished. It is founded on three great principles,—self-abnegation, obedience, and labor. It was well said of the two great leaders in the ascetic movement, "Anthony had shown the foundation of individual freedom in self-conquest; Saint Benedict showed the foundation of social freedom in self-surrender." And so their very principles of life had a marked bearing upon the social and political problems men had to work out in those hard days, and helped toward a better order than that which was so rapidly crumbling away in ruin. These communities of men knit together by ties of brotherhood, peaceful in the midst of wars, quiet and harmonious in the midst of plotting and intrigue and feuds, chaste and frugal in ages which were dying with the diseases of excess and impurity, exercised a mighty and salutary influence over the centuries in which they throve and labored. Every student knows the service the monasteries rendered to the cause of letters. Hallam well says that religion alone made a bridge across the chaos and linked the two periods of ancient and modern civilization. But the very bulwark of religion through these years was the monasteries, appearing in every community and influencing every class. Within their walls was done the only study of these years, and there was preserved the purity of the Latin tongue, which was for these times the sole hope of literature. The monasteries were the repositories for books, too, and all our manuscripts have been preserved to us in this wise, and could scarcely have come down in any other way.

To these benefits which the monastic orders were conferring on their times Saint Benedict added another when he introduced a radical change into the life of the recluse and made it an essential of the Benedictine rule that the monks should labor with their hands. Now for the first time monasticism became industrious. "Laziness," declared Benedict, " is the enemy of the soul, and therefore the brethren should at certain times occupy themselves in manual labor, at others in holy reading." And so he instituted the rule "Pray and Labor." As a result of this reform the Benedictines became the universal farmers of Europe. Wherever the convent appeared fields waved with corn and fruits ripened in autumn; and whenever the missionary went out from one of these communities into the wild land of the barbarians, he took his farmer's lore with him, and his converts became almost surely the profitable tillers of the soil. And we shall always owe it as a debt of gratitude to the monks, and especially to the Benedictines, that in an age when war was an almost universal pursuit, and all the excitements and demoralizations of a period of violence and bloodshed made men restless under the yoke of drudging toil and scornful of the plough and the axe, these men's lives were a constant example of industry and a perpetual plea in behalf of the dignity of labor.

But of course, as the Benedictines grew, they became powerful, proud, and then corrupt. That is the history of almost every human institution.

> "This is the moral of all human tales
> 'T is but the same rehearsal of the past,
> First Freedom and then Glory; when that fails,
> Wealth, Vice, Corruption."

Other orders grew up to rebuke the laxness of the monks of Saint Benedict and to reform the abuses in monastic life which had grown up with the years. And so almost simultaneously about the thirteenth century sprung up the two orders of mendicant or "begging friars." It was their aim by poverty to put away the temptations which seduced the older order from its high aims and to induce energetic labor. And these men became the street and field preachers of their times. They went about rousing the dormant religious life of the people. They were the Methodists of the thirteenth century, and their austere and consecrated lives beyond a doubt revived the power of the monks, and prolonged the day of usefulness of monasticism.

Now has not enough been shown of the character of the monks and of their system to call for a reversal of that popular prejudice which has nothing but contempt for the principles which moved them or for the work they did? It is the fashion to despise monasticism and think of a hermit or a monk as a man too weak or too cowardly to cope with the evils of his time, and who therefore, to save and shield himself, retreats to the safety of solitude, and turns his back upon a world he will not try to help. But such a thought does little justice to the motives or to the character of the hermits and the monks. It might apply to one who should make such a retreat to-day. It does not apply to the men who fled the awful vices of the most corrupt and demoralized period in history to save themselves and what remnant of their fellows they were able. These men, and especially the monks, adopted their mode of life, not as a selfish device to spare themselves from effort or from pain, but as the best means of bringing to bear the forces of religion on an evil generation; and they rallied about their order the truest, the bravest, the purest life, not only in the Church, but in all mediæval society. They stood up stoutly for law and for order in a period of tumult and of war. They held fast to literature and learning, when others were drifting into the night of ignorance and illiteracy. They tilled the soil and drained the fens of Europe. They protected the poor and withstood the oppressor. Truly he who reads the history of the great religious orders must close the book not with the feeling that he has been reading the record of fanaticism and of weakness, but with a large respect for the wisdom, the courage, and the personal force which devised a bulwark against the devastating flood of a corrupted social life, and held the ground on which in better days should be reared a finer social structure.

For ten centuries the monastic fraternities were the strength of the Church. They gathered within themselves the best life of Europe; in an age of depravity they stood for purity; in a decaying civilization they nourished a life fresh and stalwart. If you kindle at the hardy virtues of your ancestors of the North, Viking or Norseman, Saxon or Dane, remember this,— that side by side with the barbarian you must rank this cowled figure who met him with a courage equal to his own, who tamed his excesses, who set a bound to his iconoclasms, and who converted him to the religion of Christ. The monk and the Viking met in the North, and when they were done with each other, the rover of the seas was a retainer of the cross.

IV.

THE PRELATES AND THE KNIGHTS.

AMEND your lives, ye who would fain
The order of the knights attain.
Devoutly watch, devoutly pray,
From pride and sin, oh, turn away!
Shun all that 's base, the Church defend;
Be the widow's and the orphan's friend;
Be good and leal; take naught by might;
Be bold, and guard the people's right.
This is the rule for gallant knight.
                    EUSTACHE DÉSCHAMPS.

The best school of moral discipline which the Middle Ages afforded was the institution of chivalry. — HALLAM.

The papal hierarchy, in fact, instituted in the Middle Ages the main bond among the various European nations after the decline of the Roman sway; and in this view the Catholic influence ought to be judged, as De Maistre truly remarked, not only by the ostensible good which it produced, but yet more by the imminent evil which it silently obviated. — COMTE.

IV.

THE PRELATES AND THE KNIGHTS.

IT chanced one day that Saint Thomas Aquinas was sitting in the Vatican with Pope Innocent the Fourth, when great sums of silver and gold were being carried into the Papal treasury. "You see," said the Pope, with great complacency, "the age of the Church is past when she could say with Saint Peter, 'silver and gold have I none.'" "Yes," answered Thomas, "and the day also is past when she could say to the paralytic, 'Take up thy bed and walk.'"

The incident illustrates the strength and the weakness of the days on which we now come, in the development of Christendom and the changing type of the Christian ideal. For with the advent of the dark ages the Christian character and faith were doubly tried. We have seen how Christian men sought to meet the evils of the times, as these assailed their inward lives; and how, strange and extreme as their remedy appears, it did not come out of weakness in character, but out of strength and the courage to take stringent measures for the extirpation of the social vices. By self-mortification, by withdrawal from the world, by the organization of the religious orders for the rectification of society, the effort of the hermits and monks, badly as it may have found utterance according to modern standards, nevertheless expressed a form of struggle which is perpetual and which always trains tough and sinewy souls. The struggles of those early hermits, the tasks they undertook, and the work they accomplished display character cast in the heroic mould and reflecting no uncertain lustre upon the Christian name. And now we turn to another phase in the life of these same centuries. We note the call made upon the resources of the Christian character, working itself out into life and action in a dark and tumultuous period. We shall see how bravely that call was met, how entirely adequate was the new type of moral life for the new emergency, and how unabated was the vigor and the effectiveness of manhood under the tutelage of the now dominant faith.

We shall have, at the outset, to discharge from our minds a common, almost universal prejudice. It is the habit of men and women in these times to carry their antipathy against the Romish Church back to the years prior to the Reformation, and look at the early centuries, when the Papacy was rising to power, with all the acrimony born of the great religious revolution of the sixteenth century. The result is an inevitable failure to value the work done in the dark ages and mediæval times as it deserves. It was an imperfect age, and the Church and its adherents were as far below the standard of this age as ours will be to future comers on the earth. But it was not the unredeemed epoch that some men suppose; and the struggles of the time, far from being the selfish efforts of narrow bigots to serve their own personal ends, were the vigorous and wise battles of far-sighted statesmen to establish salutary institutions in a world pretty much given over to chaos. The ecclesiasticism of the Church in those days was a blessing and not a bane. It was a new form of personal force. It was another disguise of the protean and eternal energy which it is one of the functions of the gospel to foster and to unfold.

The historian of modern civilization makes this assertion concerning the Christian Church in its relations to the break-up of the Empire and the downfall of its institutions and states: "Had not the Church then existed, the whole world must have been a victim to brute force." To understand fully what this means, we must remember in what remnants the wreck of the Roman Empire left society. From the fifth to the ninth century European states were thoroughly disorganized. States, kingdoms, empires, were made and unmade with a frequency which caused the nation to seem the least stable of institutions. The boundary lines between states wavered like the shifting sea-sands. There were no central authorities for men to rally upon, no permanence to institutions, no solid ground for the expectation of security or of tranquillity. The people of Europe were like the survivors of a shipwreck, struggling in the waters in which their ship has foundered. Every man was trying to secure a piece of the wreckage big enough to save himself. Of course in such a struggle every man's hand was against his brother. The strongest arm was the ruling arm, and superior physical power was really the basis of the great re-organization of society which took place under the system of Feudalism. The castles whose grim ruins frown from the heights of Europe are the relics of the order which replaced the great central power of Rome and broke into ten thousand petty sceptres the fasces of imperial rule. Under its sway the feudal baron was the representative of kingship in his domain. He defended and governed his tenants, while they fought his battles and did his work. That, in a nutshell, was feudalism, — the half-way house of civilization, midway between the disintegration of the old Roman period and the unity of modern times. It resolved society into a multitude of petty states; or rather, it gathered up the fragments of society into these little kingdoms. But it officered these with dukes, earls, and counts; and these, by their mutual jealousies and clashing interests, kept up a perpetual warfare. It fostered the caste spirit, and so bred the evils of a serfdom which was very near to slavery. Feudalism was better than the disorders it replaced. Yet the continual wars with which the rival nobles harassed one another were but little less exhausting than the wars of the emperors; and even if the people were not formally reduced to slavery, they were treated with the same insolence and rigor as if they had been remanded to that degradation. Feudalism grew to be an estate bad alike for master and for man; it made the ruler hard, cruel, wanton, and warlike; it made the serf sullen, degraded, vindictive. "My man is mine, to boil or roast him if I will," was an old proverb, and it fully expresses the scorn and the brutal pride of power which the lord felt toward his serf. On the other hand, the groan of an oppressed and over-burdened class may be heard in the sayings which echoed for generations and centuries through Europe. "The lords would tax our light, and air, and rain." "Good people," cried John Ball, "by what right are they we call lords greater than we? Why do they hold us in serfage? It is of us and of our toil that these men hold the soil."

> "When Adam delved and Eve span,
> Where was then the gentleman?"

This much it is needful to say of the social and political conditions under the feudal system in order to describe the new ideal of courage and of positive manhood which was developed within the lines of Christendom. This was the society in which the Church was growing to a great and unprecedented power. It was the society in which was formed a new type of strength and of courage.

For we are not to think of the priestly orders, the prelates and the monks of the Church, as quietly housing themselves in abbey and monastery and isolating themselves altogether from the life of men outside. The great religious orders by their very strength and extent, were forced to become active participants in the social changes and tendencies of the age, and they were at this time the salt which savored, if it did not even save, society. The Church through its monastic institutions was the great conservative power in the world. In an age marked by the conflict of laws and authorities and the perpetual strife of powers, it enforced the supreme authority of the Divine Law as embodied in the visible powers of Holy Church. It strove to increase its influence among men. It saw its opportunity for asserting even an absolute authority, and claimed no less a prerogative over all human states. It insisted that its own rule was sovereign over subjects, lords, princes, kings, and emperors. It summoned the sanctities of religion to enforce its claims. It interfered with governments and put its own mandates above all other decrees. If any man or any government refused to do its bidding it claimed the right to destroy the rebel from the face of the earth. That in brief was the policy the Church elaborated for five centuries, till, in the time of Hildebrand, the Church really ruled the world.

Nor was this altogether the worst thing that could have happened, albeit, in a later age it became the root of abuses and of political evils. Guizot's saying certainly seems a just summary of the work of the Church in this period, when he declares that it was all that kept the world from utter wreck by brute force. Its power increased. It sought that increase, but even its strenuous effort to reach absolute power was the inevitable tendency of the only strong institution in a society full of weak devices for the maintenance of peace and order. The Church grew so strong because its strength was needed; and its career was encouraged and fostered by the belief in its high aims and endeavors. Men had faith in the Church, and that faith was based on a knowledge of what the Church was doing for the world.

It was in the development of this strength of rule that the Church formed in its adherents a new type of heroism. It is a mistake to think of Christianity as embodying itself in any fixed, formal, and inflexible type. It does not from age to age tend always to the same ends nor seek always the same ideals. We have seen how, in various epochs, the type of character which was produced under its influence was modified by the characteristics of surrounding society. This has been one secret of the power of Christianity,—that it is versatile and adapts itself to the conditions of each age in which it is at work. So now we come to a new phase of the courage, the intrepidity, the perseverance, and the strength of Christianity, in considering its attitude toward the social world for the thousand years which marked the growth of the papacy.

Consider the attitude of the Church toward the manifestations of force. Its inflexible aim during this period of unrest and social ferment was to secure mercy, justice, pity, and care for all men. It recognized no difference between the soul of the strong and the soul of the weak; and so, wherever a cruel lord abused his serf, the monk, who was everywhere, felt it his duty as the Church's representative to interfere, protest against the act, and prevent it if he could. And he entered his protest and used his influence against the more general cruelties of war. Gibbon notes the interposition of Gregory the Great to check the abuse of popular elections, and reminds us how this great ecclesiastic made the poor his special care, dealing out his treasure to supply their want and exercising his power to restrain their oppressors. The clergy possessed the right of interceding for criminals or oppressed persons; the churches became the asylums for fugitives, into which the secular authorities could not go. The priests and monks undertook the censorship of morals over those who were amenable to no other authority. Whole fraternities were formed under the inspiration of the Church to reconcile foes to one another, and one of the conditions of entering a Christian brotherhood of builders, in the Middle Ages, was that the candidate must confess and be at peace with his enemy. Peace associations were formed and funds raised as a sort of insurance against damage by violence of war; laws were passed forbidding men to travel with arms, or to do violence to peasants, serfs, or clerks. In all these lines of work and influence, the Church was centuries in advance of the civil authorities, and set the example of what had to be done, and what was done finally, over all Europe.

But we must not suppose that this task which the Church set for itself was one which cost nothing and called for no courage and strength. For the priest to face the petty lord, for the bishop or the archbishop to confront dukes, princes, kings, maintaining his principle and insisting on his humane claims, often required the same courage that men need on the field of battle or to bear martyrdom. Secular authority was arrogant, irritable, and violent, and the habit of monk or priest was no shield against hatred or hostility. And so the inheritance of courage which had borne Christianity forward through all obstacles down to this age was passed on, changed only in the mode of its exercise, to this new generation.

Perhaps the most striking triumph of the Church in these ages was the establishment of what was called the Peace of God. The clergy, being unable in that warlike time to secure all the year for peaceful pursuits, induced the wild barons to admit certain days, places, and pursuits as inviolable and sacred to peace. The holy days, the feasts and other Christian festivals, such as Christmas, Easter, and the time in each week covering the days of the Passion, were set apart as days in which wars should not be waged nor the people disturbed in their peaceful pursuits. By this law the peasants were guarded, and the cart, grain, and cattle of the farmer made as sacred as the utensils of the Church itself; and all this was enforced by the threat of excommunication, the most dreadful ban of the Church. Thus the Church stood for gentleness and peace. Her power was reared as a barrier against the rude and turbulent seas of human passion, which beat upon all institutions in those stormy times. All along our eastern coast are harbors, great and small, land-locked, protected by island, headland, or cape, into whose smooth waters the craft that skirt our coast on their busy errands of commerce may run if beset by storms and find smooth waters, good anchorage, care, and safety. The arm of land stretches between them and the sea they have escaped, — a rampart of protection. So the institutions of the Church, her laws and her prerogatives, were stretched for ages between the weaker classes and the turbulence of an unsettled time of oppressions, and whoever sought refuge behind her power was protected and saved.

One more fact will illustrate the vigor of the Church's life and the courage and steadfastness of her monks and clergy.

This was her stern and unswerving cultivation of the spirit of equality. The Church set her face steadfastly against the spirit of caste, which was the life of Feudalism, and this attitude was heroically maintained. In her ranks all human distinctions were levelled; she made men brethren indeed. Her services were equally at the call of all men; her offices were open to all comers. A pope chosen from among the nobility might be succeeded by a cobbler's son. The Church was as thorough a democracy in this respect as our own land, whose highest office is open to the aspirant from the lowest station. Prince and peasant were absolutely on a level. Louis, the son of Charlemagne, set the example for sovereigns in all coming times, when he thrice prostrated himself before Pope Stephen IV. It was a later custom for the prince to hold the bridle-rein of a pope when the pontiff mounted his horse. "This theory of equality on a level absolutely independent of family or rank was vividly presented to the eye when a weak old man, small of stature and lean with long fasting, claiming to own not a farthing of worldly wealth, forbidden the use of any violence, saw at his feet the proudest of feudal lords, — when Hildebrand saw Henry of Germany doing him reverence at Canossa."

The mention of this name calls to mind the triumph of the prelates in their struggles with the social forces with which they had engaged. The attitude of the leaders of Christendom, their power over social tendencies, the influence they had not hesitated to exert in the face of all violence and hostility of a warlike age, had fostered their power, and human-like, they craved more, and it became the dream of one man to establish not alone the entire independence of the Church but its authority over the temporal sovereigns. That man was Hildebrand, the son of an Italian carpenter, educated in a monastery at Rome, and afterward a monk at Cluny in France. By chance the newly chosen Pope, Leo IX., stopped at Cluny on his way to take his seat, — a providence, not a chance, — and meeting this thin, fiery, fanatical man, full of theories and plans and devices, was so impressed with him that he begged him to go in his retinue to Rome. Hildebrand went on condition that the Pope would journey as a pilgrim. He became his advisor, "Lord of our Lord the Pope," and during Leo's reign and that of four successors, kept his hand on the helm, until he himself was chosen pope as Gregory VII. His twelve years' reign left an impress on the Church's policy which eight hundred years have not worn off.

Two things Hildebrand aimed to do and did. First, he concentrated and established the power of the clergy. He showed all the courage of a Luther in reform, though with a less rational theory. He aimed to purge the Church of abuses and purify its life, and to do this involved in his view two great undertakings; first, to forbid the marriage of the clergy; secondly, to abolish the purchase and sale of livings and places in the Church. In both of these attempts Hildebrand encountered the vigorous opposition of his subordinates, but showed inflexible determination and an energy which persisted to success. Secondly, he asserted and established the absolute supremacy of the Church over the State. The prelates had hitherto held offices owning a double allegiance, one to the Pope, and one to the king or emperor. The same man was thus both an ecclesiastical and a civil magistrate. But Gregory insisted that every bishop, no matter of what land, must receive the crosier, ring, and staff from him and not from the sovereign; no priest must accept these emblems at the hands of a layman. That was the blow which struck at the State and which would put half the property of Europe into the control of the Pope. No wonder that this move raised a turmoil through the whole Christian world. Hildebrand did not live to see his purpose carried into full effect; he died in exile, a victim of Henry IV., whom he had humiliated. But his work went on, and in the reign of Alexander III., at Venice, Frederick Barbarossa prostrated himself before the Pope in token of submission. Three porphyry slabs in St. Mark's Portico mark the place where this triumph was consummated; and a century later, at a great Christmas jubilee, Pope Boniface III. summoned all Christendom to attend, and as he marched to the High Altar two swords were borne before him, as a symbol of the power, both temporal and spiritual, which it was the privilege of that one hand to wield.

It is doubtful if we appreciate the true proportions of the courage and energy displayed in this struggle between the Church and the State. For one reason, because we do not sympathize with the end for which it was put forth; for another because the courage of the diplomat or the statesman, being quieter in its exercise and less obtrusive, does not compare well in the popular esteem with the bravery which wins battles or endures the rack or the stake. But unquestionably Christendom owes great thanks to the steadfast perseverance of the prelates and their unflinching faithfulness to their ideals. They were true to their own best light; they were equal to the emergencies of their age; they were the equals of the rough fighters whom they restrained and conquered. All honor to priest and monk, who, in a day when these names meant more than they do in the nineteenth century, moved by the old spirit of Justin, Anthony, and Saint Francis, once more confronted the new evils of a new age, to conquer and control them!

It would be an omission of one of the most important effects in the improvement of manners and of morals if we failed to dwell upon the influence and the achievements of the various orders of knighthood, and the spirit of chivalry, which through the Middle Ages materially helped the Church in its struggle against the world, and illustrated afresh the power of Christian heroism. It is not difficult to explain the origin of the spirit of chivalry. It was the outgrowth of the Crusades. The rise of the Mohammedans and their possession of the Holy City and sepulchre filled Christian hearts with grief. The preaching of Peter the hermit summoned a great horde of princes, knights, armies, and followers, who for two hundred years, in successive expeditions sought to win back into Christian hands the spots so dear to Christian hearts. We may say it was a sentimental strife, the outgrowth of pure passion turned by crafty priests into a means of advancing the power of the Church; but we must remember at least that it was undertaken with devoutness of purpose, and prosecuted with a heroism worthy of a better cause, and with a patience sometimes as sweet as martyrdom itself.

The Crusades and the struggle for papal

supremacy were two battles for ideals which we must count wrong and demoralizing, but incidentally they held in check and modified the harsh and turbulent elements of feudal life; they tempered Christendom with a new and kindlier spirit; they illustrated afresh the manly vigor of Christian hearts; they added their quota to the great army who exemplified that Christian heroism, which, however it may vary in type, is the same in spirit through all ages.

For out of the Crusades came the institution of chivalry, the prophecy of the day when strength shall wed with grace and power with love, the unfulfilled promise of the time when self-sacrifice shall take the place of this world's self-seeking, and men strive in the rivalry of a generous service to their kind. The character of a true knight, at once pious and valorous, strong in arm and tender in heart, is a creation of Christianity; nor has Christianity on the whole produced any finer type.

It needs no argument to prove that chivalry was a clear type of the courage and manly virtue which may exist under Christian training. The ideal was created by the union of the martial spirit with the

Christian virtues. It demanded justice, courtesy, and respect for woman. In these great requirements, however narrowly they were held and however poorly realized, Christian men laid the foundations for a broader and better type of manliness than had ever been witnessed before on earth. And in these conditions that it set up as the characteristics of an ideal were disclosed a triple courage and strength. For in this ideal Christian men encountered the three great evils of the times. When they insisted on justice, they aimed a blow at all the oppressions great and small which made life burdensome; and when they demanded courtesy they put a ban upon the all but universal cruelties, rudeness, violence which turned society into one great brawl; and in calling for reverence for woman they attacked that traditional tyranny of the physically stronger sex over the weaker, which only now begins to draw to an end. We are accustomed to dwell upon chivalry as the dawn of the spirit of refinement in the secular character which marks how far the Christian spirit has penetrated the every-day standards of humanity; but we are never at liberty to forget that it was a refinement whose basis was courage, a grace whose root was in manly strength, a consideration for the weak born of a high sense of the obligations of power.

We have the legacy of chivalry in "the grand old name of gentleman" and the ideal it suggests. Dissociate that term from all the foolish traditions with which society has hung it about; use it in the simple ethical sense in which it means most to most men and women; drop all the fopperies and artificialities and follies which unworthy minds have tacked upon it to make it fit small men, mean men, contemptible men, and you will have in what is left a noble embodiment of the highest type of manhood which Christian principles have grafted upon the sturdy stock of the natural man. With true perception of the large inheritance that word derives from the side of manly strength, Juliana Berners says, in the quaint phrase of the "Heraldic Blazonry," "Of the offspring of the gentilman Jafeth came Habraham, Moyses, Aron and the profettys; and also the Kyng of the right lyne of Mary, of whom that gentilman

Jhesus was borne." With equal insight into the gracious and refined qualities which make it the fit designation of our regenerate manhood, a later writer has declared, "A Christian is God Almighty's gentleman."

When the monitor "Tecumseh" on that August morning in Mobile Bay was running the rebel forts, she was rent by a torpedo and went down with all on board. "It was then," says the historian, "that [her commander] Craven did one of those deeds that should always be linked with the doer's name, as Sidney's is with the cup of cold water. The pilot and he instinctively made for the narrow opening leading to the turret below. Craven drew back. 'After you, pilot,' he said. There was no afterward for him; the pilot was saved, but he went down with his ship." There was a lineal descendant of the elder knighthood and the true type of the hero for all time to come, the full fruit of a manly strength ripened in the sunshine of the Christian spirit.

V.

THE REFORMERS.

8

YE are the light of the world. A city that is set on a hill cannot be hid. — *Matt.* v. 14.

The Church of Rome is seen under Leo X. in all its strength and glory. A monk speaks, — and in the half of Europe, this power and glory suddenly crumble into dust. — D'AUBIGNÉ.

>   Life may be given in many ways,
>   And loyalty to truth be sealed
>   As bravely in the closet as the field,
>   So bountiful is Fate;
>   But then to stand beside her,
>   When craven churls deride her,
>   To front a lie in arms and not to yield,
>   This shows, methinks, God's plan
>   And measure of a stalwart man,
>   Limbed like the old heroic breeds.
>   LOWELL: *Commemoration Ode.*

My poor monk, thou hast a march and a struggle to go through such as neither I nor many other captains have seen the like in our most bloody battles. — GEORGE VON FREUNDSBERG (to Luther).

V.

THE REFORMERS.

THE Christian Church has always furnished its own reformers. Whenever in its changeful history errors and abuses have crept into its life, and the very principles by which it lives and thrives have been denied in the practice of those who use its name and profess its creed, the power of Christ's spirit has raised up souls to correct the abuses and recall men to the fundamentals of the faith. The forward movements of the Church have always been led by men whom she herself has trained; and however wrong the majority may sometimes have gone, there has always been a healthy and vigorous minority, though sometimes indeed only a minority of one ready to halt in the path and stand there until the march of the Church has been turned back to the right way. And in these exploits of reform, in these renewals of the moral rectitude of Christendom, have been displayed some of the finest efforts of courage, strength, and manliness that this world has ever witnessed.

It is to the career and work of some of these souls that we now turn. We take up the history of the men, who, born in the Church, trained in its institutions, and bred to its best spirit, revolted against its corruptions, recovered its pure traditions, and brought it back to the honest purpose of its earliest days. And as the great movements which culminated in the Reformation were scattered over many lands and prolonged for over two centuries, it will best serve our purpose of illustration if we touch upon the lives of several of the most eminent of these Christian heroes, who made the modern world as you and I know it not only a possibility but also a reality. John Wyclif, John Huss, Jerome Savonarola, and Martin Luther,— an Englishman, a Bohemian, a Florentine, and a German.

In naming the cause of the Reformation it is needless to rehearse the familiar story of the growth of corruption and the decay of spiritual prestige in the Church. It has been shown how pure and how earnest the Church really was all through the dark ages, and how firm a bulwark to the feeble and demoralized remnants of society struggling for life against the attacks of hostile and deadly forces. The Church in all these times stood for equality in the face of the caste spirit which grew up under feudalism. It stood for protection to the weak in an age when brute force wreaked its most savage will upon the feeble and defenceless; it upheld learning and education amidst the densest ignorance and deadness of intellectual life; and it held unflinchingly to the supremacy of the spiritual in the midst of a society which was sunk in superstition and mindful only of the coarsest and most material forces and laws. If it usurped a power and a place not meet for it to hold, it was only as men in emergencies are called to do what they are not fitted to do, what they shrink from doing, but what they alone can do and must do. And no prejudice against what the Church came to be in its days of corruption and self-stultification ought to blind us to the essential excellence and necessity of the work it did when it became the conservator and the guardian of society. "Never," says Froude, "in all their history . . . have men thrown out of themselves anything so grand, so beautiful, so useful, as this Catholic Church once was. . . . At this time the Church ruled the State with the authority of conscience." It was a brave and noble work which the Church was doing with the world in those days; and the men and women who were brought up in the influences of the Christian faith were the strongest and the most conspicuous among all the leaders of their times.

But the papacy was destined to a downfall. It was cherishing in itself the seeds of its own dissolution. The old order served its purpose and did its work; and then it was time for it to give place to a new one. There were three great causes which overthrew the temporal power of the Church and brought on a complete revolution in society.

The first was the rivalry of powers in Europe. During the same centuries which witnessed the increase of the Church's power in Europe, three great nations had been forming out of the wreckage and the remnants of the Empire. England rose to a commanding position in the affairs of the continent; France acquired glory and rank under the administration of Charlemagne; and Germany had already grown to a strength which made her the formidable rival of the other two. And naturally, as these great powers became conscious of their own strength and jealous of external powers, they grew restive under the control of this foreign ecclesiastical principality. The German could ill brook the interference of an Italian or a Spaniard who from his throne at Rome dictated the emperor's policy. It went hard with Englishmen to see the Pope's collector at London send off from time to time thousands of guineas in good English gold to put into these foreign coffers. There could be but one end to these jealousies and suspicions. They all tended to the overthrow of the temporal authority of Rome.

Another contributing cause was the revival of learning. The intellect of Europe was awakening. There was great stir in the world of discovery, of letters, and of the arts. The realm of men's knowledge was enlarging and the courage and independence of their thoughts were increasing. Copernicus created the new astronomy. Columbus opened the way to the New World. Gutenberg invented the most important art ever given to the human race since it learned the use of fire. In England scholarship grew with the centuries and a literature developed from Chaucer to Shakspeare. In Italy the splendors of the Renaissance were heightened by the light of the glorious names of the great artists Leonardo and Titian, Raphael and Michael Angelo. It was a wonderful period in the world's history, and out of it came the most radical steps in the reformation of old abuses and the abolition of old evils.

These changes were hastened so far as the Church was concerned by the corruption and the absolutism of the papacy. Too much power and too complete absorption in worldly concerns had eaten out the earnestness of the Church. The old spirit of denial and self-mortification had given place to greed and pride, and carnality and lust of power. The Church had come too close to the State and had been defiled. The mercenary spirit prevailed among priests and prelates alike, and the Church was everywhere permitting its officials to beg of all men and lay society under a perpetual money-tribute for the benefit of its treasury. The administration of religion became an organized system of plunder. Preferment in the Church was openly bought and sold; and so profound was the degradation of the Church's moral sense that she permitted the awful blasphemy to be taught that for a sum of money a full discharge might be purchased from the penalties of sin and the release of a soul secured from the flames of purgatory. The consequences of such a prostitution of religion may be imagined. And when the sentiment began to be general that the policy of the Church was venal, debasing, the end was near. When Luther could voice a general feeling in his words, " Everything is permitted at Rome but to be an honest man," it was not far to rebellion against the power that fostered such abuses.

These were the three great causes of

that religious revolution which took the half of Europe from the Pope's control, and whose continuing force has pushed that functionary from one stronghold to another, until at last he is shut up to a political jurisdiction over the scanty grounds of the Vatican Palace. And if the men who began this work of moral regeneration within the Church had been permitted to foresee the results of their work, it would have been a mighty and cheering inspiration. But even then the task before them would have been one to appall any but the most stout-hearted. It called for the most unflinching and steadfast qualities to begin and to carry on the tremendous struggle which now for two hundred years shook Europe and reached all hearts within its borders; and the men who prepared the ground for Protestant Christianity were the worthy successors in all heroic qualities of the generations of Christian hearts which had preceded them. They displayed all the old courage of the early martyrs, and the same sturdy faithfulness to the truth as faced the superstition and bigotry of the Empire and upheld the doctrines of the faith once committed to the saints. "Play the man, Master Ridley," cried old Bishop Latimer, when Bloody Mary dragged them from their prison to die at the stake; "Play the man, and we shall this day light such a candle in England as shall never be put out!" That was the stuff which was in these modern martyrs, these new defenders of the faith, these children of the brave old hermits, the priests and knights, with all the chivalry of the elder days still fresh in their souls.

In the middle of the fourteenth century England was full of gloom and agitation. The Black Death, the most terrible plague that the world had ever witnessed, had swept down upon England, and one half the population of the kingdom became its victims; the industrial system begot misery, discontent, and revolt among the laboring class; the costly campaigns of the king involved the nation in most exacting taxation; and to crown all, the dissatisfaction of the people flamed up in a bitter hate of the friars, the prelates, and the papacy. It was in such an hour that there appeared in England a man who was destined to rank as the forerunner of the

Reformation, and anticipate by a century and a half the work of Martin Luther. John Wyclif, whose name is always to be associated with the English Bible, which he first of all Englishmen translated into the mother-tongue, was the man who almost single-handed attacked the creed and the practice of the Church and asserted the freedom of religious thought against the papacy. He was a thin, spare man, quick and restless, with untiring energy and undaunted courage. He was an Oxford graduate and conspicuous for his learning. But he stood by the common people as their sympathizer and as their advocate; and when a controversy arose between Edward III. and the Pope, Wyclif took the most positive stand against the exactions of Rome, and in resistance to the exorbitant demands of the Holy See. It was not long before Wyclif became a conspicuous figure in England in the struggle to be rid of papal supremacy. He grew strong with the controversies in which he engaged. His mind broadened; his courage against the popes increased. He began to see what others were faintly perceiving, that the papal system was not essential to the life of Christianity; that it was not necessarily the Church; and that very possibly all that passed as orthodox and heaven-ordained might not be either. His search for the fundamentals of Christianity led him back to the Bible, and he determined that it ought to be in the power of every man to read his Bible in the mother-tongue. That was the motive which impelled him to the great work of his life, the translation of the Bible into English, that it might be within the reach of every Englishman. "The sacred Scriptures" he held "to be the property of the people, and one which no party should be allowed to wrest from them." He soon accomplished his desire, and his translation of the Bible was the first ever made into English, being the basis of the Book Englishmen read to-day. This was the great and lasting influence of John Wyclif, a Protestant one hundred and fifty years before Luther and a Puritan three hundred years before Cromwell. And as one reads the story of his life-work, one feels that he had in him all the aggressive energy of his countrymen; all the courage and determination which had brought order out of the chaos of kingdoms which made England; all the dogged sense of right and determination to have it which had gained Magna Charta; all the instinct for freedom which restrained kings and forced concessions from nobles, till English liberty blossomed into the great republic of the west. Yet this was a man whose Christian training was bestowed on a heart disposed to the ideals of the cross. And here, thirteen hundred years after Calvary, comes a hero to show us how unabated was the aggressive fighting spirit in the hearts of those who inherited the Christian name. Nothing is lost from the old force, — we only see it glorified with a nobler motive and trained up to a larger strength.

But Wyclif's influence did not die with him. He was too great a man to be shut up to the limits of England. His following there was large, and his principles swept over into the Continent and made themselves new friends. There was a nickname which began now to be heard in England which concentrated in itself something of the hate and scorn that used to hiss in the word "abolitionist." It was the term "Lollard," which was given to Wyclif's followers as they took up the practice of street-preaching, that they might the more easily counteract the work of the begging friars. The spirit of Wyclif, reinforced by the social discontent, the hatred of the barons toward the priests, the new demand for purer living, made its way everywhere. The new sect was omnipresent, and in its one great tenet, a faith in the sole authority of the Bible as the word of truth, was the prophecy of the coming struggle. To be of this hated name, to call one's self a Lollard, to believe that a layman was free to read the Bible, to preach these heresies openly, was to incur persecution and martyrdom. But in such an age and among such hearts martyrdom is but fuel to feed the fires of conviction and sacrifice. The movement passed over the Channel from England. It spread on the Continent. It attracted the attention of devout and sincere churchmen everywhere, and it reached among others the attention of John Huss, a Bohemian of the city of Prague. For years the clergy of that city had been preaching against the corruptions of the Church and denying the divine origin of the hierarchy which had established itself at Rome. The soil was prepared for the seed which Wyclif had been sowing, and the Bohemian reformer insisted with an ominous persistency upon the principles which were destined one day to split the Church. In a day of the centralization of power and the support of religion by taxes and tribute, John Huss advanced the doctrines of congregationalism and the voluntary support of worship. These were bold things to advocate in a time when to question the authority of the Church was to invite the exercise of that authority against one's self, but Huss did a still bolder. When Pope John XXIII., to raise money for his war against Naples, offered indulgences for sale, Huss burned the papal bull at the public pillory, denouncing the whole proceeding as wicked and unwarrantable. That does not seem so much, perhaps, to us, who enjoy all the fruits of the freedom of conscience these men bought for us, but it was a daring and heroic act. Christian men, priests of the Holy Church, were not allowed such latitude of action in those times, and most heroically was

John Huss to answer for it. He was summoned to Constance to explain his heresies or to retract them. He went under pledge of safe conduct, but the Church did not consider it necessary to keep faith with infidels, and so he was seized and imprisoned. He was cruelly executed in 1415, but not until he had given a new impulse to the life which was starting in the veins of Europe. It was the hand of Huss that passed the torch of the Reformation on from Wyclif to Luther.

But while these influences were abroad in England and in Germany they were not wanting elsewhere. Italy was alive. The revival of learning had affected no land more brilliantly, and the free cities with their republican spirit and governments were ripening for revolt against the now overgrown papacy; and in Florence, the richest of all these cities, the rebellion flamed up into open defiance. Here in this opulent city, famed in all Europe as it is in all later ages for its distinctions in art, in political liberty, in wealth, and in magnificence, lived and died one of the truest and boldest hearts the Church ever claimed.

Jerome Savonarola was a true reformer. He spared no sin of his city or her citizens. He sought with all the intensity of a sincere nature to purify his Church of her corruptness; and his career is one more of those brilliant examples of the inspiration which the Christian faith gives to bold hearts to put forth all their strength and live out all the native force there is within them. He was a preacher at the famous church of Saint Mark's, and like almost every other man of note in those ages, a member of a monastic order, being a Dominican friar. From the pulpit of the popular church he poured forth his fiery denunciations of the sinfulness of Florence. His utterances carried more weight than those of any man in Florence, and he used his influence to promote pure living and consecrated hearts. He was the favorite and the leader of the populace, and when Charles VIII. of France appeared before the walls of the city and it was betrayed into his hands, Savonarola was summoned to intercede with the king. He saved the city, and when Charles soon after left it, Savonarola was again summoned to direct affairs in the re-organization of the government. It was a little republic which he founded within the walls of Florence. This liberty-loving monk gave the people representation, and whoever loves the principles of representative government is bound to honor the memory of this Florentine priest.

But alas! there were few such souls in Italy then; few that loved freedom; few that could bear with the unsparing righteousness of an outspoken reformer. Especially was his ardor for freedom and for pure morals distasteful to the Pope, and when we have said that, we have intimated the fate of Savonarola. When a man in those days entered into a controversy with a pope, it was like arguing with the law of gravitation. In the midst of the profoundest tumult and popular discontent Savonarola was excommunicated. The tragic end of it all was deferred for a little, but it could not be averted; and when at last a summons came for him to appear before a tribunal, the end had come. He died a martyr to truth; and Martin Luther, declaring that Savonarola was a forerunner of his own teaching, says of him: "He was burned by the Pope, but he lives in blessedness, and Christianity has canonized him."

Such were the men and such the spirit which prepared the way for the religious revolution of the sixteenth century. In selecting these famous names we have taken only an example of the great movement in spirit and in thought which was in progress all through the Christian world. As yet it was a hard and a daring thing to attempt to lead that movement or to speak in its favor. It meant persecution, it meant ostracism, it meant death. And that these men and their brave followers were undeterred by the marshalled strength of Europe, the allied interests of Church and popular prejudice striving to hush their speech and intimidate their hearts, is a signal illustration and proof of the thesis we are seeking to maintain,—that the strong and aggressive virtues of manhood, which thrill, inspire, and fascinate us, have suffered no languor with the spread of the spirit of Christianity.

And now we come to the moment when, at thirty-five, Martin Luther sounded the call of the Reformation. It is so familiar that we scarce need go over the story.

The tale has been told till all men know it, how Pope Leo X., wishing to build St. Peter's according to the designs furnished by Michael Angelo, wanted large sums of money from the faithful throughout Europe. All the world knows the scandalous means which this polished ecclesiastic, this churchly gentleman, this patron of the arts, took to replenish his treasury; how he sent monks far and wide with papal dispensations and indulgences, how these were permissions to do what the Church forbade to be done, to eat meat on fast days, to marry near relations, to do any questionable act, the concession to be paid for by the merits of dead saints, "placed to the account of the delinquents by the Pope's letters in consideration of value received." It was a virtual permission to sin, with pardon granted in advance and the pardon paid for by the prospective sinner. And a Dominican monk, Tetzel by name, actually appeared one day in Wittenberg and began to peddle his singular wares in Luther's town. "Now you can ransom your souls," he cried. "Hard-hearted man, with twelve pence you can deliver your father out of purgatory. The Lord has committed all power to the Pope." And he told the people that the moment their money tinkled in his box, the soul flew out of purgatory. This was the man, a profligate monk, parading with drum and bell from town to town, who called forth the ire of Dr. Martin Luther, and precipitated the struggle that shook the world. "Please God," said Luther, "I will make a hole in that drum of his." And so he did, but not until its noisy rattle had started all Europe into an uproar.

It sometimes happens in the mountain districts, that after long and heavy rains the soil, saturated and loosened by the moisture, hangs to the bare rock underneath by the most insecure grasp and needs but the slightest shock to bring it down, with rocks, trees, and herbage, in one great crash into the valleys below. Then it is a perilous time, for the firing of a gun, the stroke of the woodman's axe, or even the shout from a human voice may set the air in vibration and start the avalanche. So all Europe hung on the verge of a landslide at the beginning of the sixteenth century. In Church, in State, in the arts, in the world of thought, society clung but loosely to the old order, was ready to slip away at any moment; and when Tetzel's drum beat in the streets of Wittenberg, the waiting air caught up its dull vibrations and rolled their echoes up the mountain-sides, till the Alps and the Apennines, the stormy fastnesses of Scandinavia and the crags of old Albion shivered and shook, and rumbled and gave back the sound in a reverberation that brought down churches and States, old systems and manners grown corrupt, burying the life and the sins of the Middle Ages in one vast ruin.

On the 31st of October, 1517, Luther nailed to the door of the Church in Wittenberg his ninety-five theses against the doctrine of indulgences. "Every Christian," they asserted, "who truly repents of his sins has entire forgiveness of the penalty and the fault, and so far has no need of indulgence. . . . The Pope cannot by his indulgence take away the smallest daily sin, in regard to the fault or delinquency." That was the gage of battle Luther flung down. It was the beginning of a tremendous debate. The defenders of the Church rushed to the rescue and strove to crush the daring man who lifted his feeble voice against a pope, and defied the authorities and the resources of the Church universal. Pope Leo heard of the trouble but pronounced it only a squabble of monks. When he saw the theses he only laughed at them in easy contempt. "A drunken German wrote them," he said, "when he has slept off his wine he will be of another mind." Various prelates tried their various arts on Luther, now persuading, now threatening, always seeking to dissuade him from his position and keep him quiet. But at all events he must retract. This man must be stopped in his course; if he went on, what would become of the monks? They could not make a living if the people thought their sins would be forgiven without the hired help of the clergy. As a great historian has said, "If souls could not be sung out of purgatory, their occupation was gone." They would have killed him if they could, as John Huss had been killed, and Jerome Savonarola, who fell in the skirmish-line of the Reformation. But a powerful and friendly **prince** stood between him and any such untoward fate. Frederick the Elector of Saxony would not consent to do anything against Luther, and without this prince no action could touch him. Then the Pope sent for him to come to Rome. But finally the Pope's legate met the contumacious monk at Wittenberg. The cardinal did everything but argue with him. He was too shrewd to do that, — Luther would have made him ridiculous. But he could remonstrate, he could threaten, he could offer bribes, he could point out the absurdity of this poor friar's defying the power of the spiritual sovereign of Christendom. But one thing he could not do. He could not turn Martin Luther from his conviction of the truth.

So the mission of the legate ended. He went home to his master. The Pope excommunicated Luther. The quarrel went on. It was a battle between a poor monk and the supreme pontiff of Christendom. There were debates, writings of pamphlets, talk among the people, ranging of men on one side or the other. At last the Pope issued another bull against Luther, and the daring man burned it in the public square at Wittenberg, and a great concourse of people looked on with shouts of approval. "It was the shout," says Carlyle, "of the awakening of nations!"

The time would fail us to trace in every detail the sequence of events which thrust Luther forward, made his great gifts manifest, and developed the Reformation. The one famous scene at Worms will never die out of history. It was in April, 1521. The Diet of the Empire assembled there, and Luther was summoned into the presence of Charles V. to defend himself. It was peril to go. He had no assurance of safety. The Church was treacherous then, and many a man had been put out of the way who dared to thwart her ministers. As Luther went thither a friend came to warn him that if he went on he was a dead man. Luther trembled. He was sensible to danger. But here his true courage appeared in his immortal answer, "I would go thither if there were as many devils in Worms as tiles on the roofs of the houses." And there before the sovereign of half Europe, before archbishops and ministers of State, before princes and knights of the realm, this poor miner's son stood up to defend himself from the charge of teaching doctrines which the Pope had pronounced false. And what was his reply? Why, simply that if they would not merely declare his doctrines false, but prove them so, he would retract, not otherwise. There was the gist of the whole Reformation. It was saying in effect that the Pope's "say so" was not enough; that nothing was true because the Pope affirmed it. It was a remarkable saying. It was simple enough. Any man might have said it. But no man had said it till Luther dared to. And when he spoke, the inflated bubble of papal authority that had glittered all through the Middle Ages, now with a splendor that almost deceived the wise into believing it solid and real, now with lurid gleams that had warned the wary of its hollowness and humbug, burst and disappeared. It was the greatest moment in modern history. The fate of Christendom hung on Luther's words. If he wavered, men might go on believing the old lies, yielding a hollow allegiance, sickening over the shams that they hated, trammelled in thought, in utterance, and in action. If he recanted, he would turn back the hour-hand of progress for centuries. But hear him! Hark to his brave words! "Here am I! God help me, I cannot otherwise!" Thank God! Thank God! brave monk, thou hast saved us. Thou hast spoken the word which opens a new age to man. Thou hast proclaimed a new day to Christianity and a new civilization to society. It is thy stanch courage which drew its strength out of the heart of the Man of Nazareth which has prevailed over the mighty. And as long as the world canonizes strength and steadfastness, thy name shall shine among the brightest of heroic souls!

In this episode we confront the most signal type of heroism which the Church has cherished. It is harder to differ from one's friends and call them to account for sins and errors than it is to turn on enemies and outsiders. It is a heavier cross to bear the coldness of the family circle than to hear the rabble without denounce or jeer. The men who from the standpoint of the Church denounced the Church, whom the Church put to death because of the good they meant to her own cause;

who suffered her anathema, and knew that after she had tortured them she would not harbor their poor bones in her tombs, all because they loved her too well to see her die in her sins, — these were among the noblest heroes she ever had. They are the choicest type of Christian heroism.

VI.

THE MISSIONARIES.

THE field is the world. — *Matt.* xiii. 38.

> With all his sufferings full in view
> And woes to us unknown,
> Forth to the task his spirit flew.
> 'T was love that urged him on.
> COWPER.

And I saw another angel fly in the midst of heaven, having the everlasting gospel to preach unto them that dwell on the earth, and to every nation and kindred and tongue and people, saying with a loud voice, Fear God and give glory to him; for the hour of his judgment is come: and worship him that made heaven and earth and sea, and the fountains of waters. — *Rev.* xiv. 6, 7.

Bestir yourselves, then, ye heroic and illustrious leaders of the army of Christ. . . . Overturn, quench, destroy, not men but ignorance, godlessness, and other sins. . . . It is hard work I call you to, but it is highest and noblest of all. — ERASMUS: *Art of Preaching*.

VI.

THE MISSIONARIES.

CHRISTIANITY is the only religion which has aimed at the conversion of the world. It was a mark of its founder's singularity among men that he avowedly planned a world-wide conquest through the preaching of his word. He entered a world which was a stranger to his name, and deliberately planned a spiritual crusade which he intended should leave him the master of the ends of the earth.

It seems to be a characteristic of the great philosophers of the world that they address themselves only to a small spiritual aristocracy, and the greater the philosopher the fewer souls he expects to touch; but this greatest of teachers reverses the principle at the very beginning. His avowed object is the conversion of the world. He aims at the hearts of all men, and most wonderful and most characteristic of all, he sets on foot a scheme which he never expects to see perfected, but which he looks to see executed only in the final harvest of the world. "This thought of a universal kingdom cemented in God," says Horace Bushnell, "why! the immense Roman Empire of his day, constructed by so many ages of war and conquest, is a bauble in comparison, both as regards the extent and the cost; and yet the rustic craftsman of Galilee propounds even this for his errand, and that in a way of assurance as simple and quiet as if the immense reach of his plan were in fact a matter to him of no consideration." The only great religious movements that ever offered even a remote resemblance in this respect to Christianity were Mohammedanism and Buddhism; but the sword of Islam, drawn to propagate a temporal and worldly power, swept only the Oriental races, and Buddhism never looked outside the farther east. Christianity alone has conceived the purpose and carried it out, of establishing its churches on every coast from the shores of Greenland to the Antarctic Circle. It aims at the spiritual dominion of the whole world. It sends its messengers to every land under the sun. It has entered upon a campaign which confessedly can only be carried out in a long series of ages; but its leaders and its workers aim at nothing less, will be content with nothing less, and already the signs point most encouragingly toward the consummation of the scheme.

One of the most interesting documents a man can study is a chart of the world's religions. It is more interesting even and more significant than a map of political geography, for it sets before the eye the signs of the great religious movements of society. It indicates the trend of faith and of spiritual life. It enables us from year to year to satisfy ourselves that this world is advancing out of paganism into Christianity. Imagine such a map to lie before you. Recall the time, nearly two thousand years ago, when the foothold of Christianity in the earth could have been covered by a needle's point on the chart, or that earlier day when there was no such thing in existence. For years after its founder's death this obscure religion was colonized in a few towns along the Mediterranean Sea.

Since then what changes have occurred! Europe, with its dense populations, owns allegiance to Jesus Christ; and stretching eastward across the continent to the Pacific, the great Russian Empire mingles with the pagan influences of the native races the name and power of Christianity. To the south and east the sturdy enterprise of Englishmen and of Americans has carried the gospel to South Africa, has half converted Madagascar, and has brought Australia and New Zealand well under the power of the cross. The dense populations of India feel the pressure of Christianity and show results not to be measured by the mere catalogue of conversions. If we turn to the west, the inspiring spectacle is presented of an entire hemisphere dominated and governed by Christian principle and thought, which run deeply into all its institutions. But that is not the most significant nor the most cheering fact to Christian men, for these conquests might be only the culmination of forces already spent, and about to decline or suffer reaction; but that we are witnesses to no such weakening of the forces which have already conquered so many millions of earth's multitudes is proved by the fact that wherever heathenism is most strongly entrenched we see the outposts of the Christian forces, encamped like a beleaguering army, advancing their lines, but never withdrawing them, year after year. Africa is belted with mission stations from Gibraltar to the Red Sea and from Sierra Leone to Zanzibar. The intrepid spirit of Livingstone has opened the heart of the Dark Continent to Europe and the influences of the cross, and already one faithful bishop has renewed the ancient story of martyrdom in the way of loving duty there. The coasts of China are fringed with missionary posts, and the islands of the South Seas are full of them. The great Empire of Japan is opening its mind and heart to Christianity, and among the uncivilized peoples of America a work is going on which cannot be put upon any map, but whose full significance can only be felt by those who have followed the noble labors of Christian philanthropy at Hampton and Carlisle. These signs all point to a vigor of spirit still unabated, a purpose fresh and earnest, a consecration which deepens as the years go by; and they all show as plainly as indications may that future when the map to the world shall be a chart of Christendom.

Now in this fact alone, standing before us in the emphasis of statistics and pictured outlines, is a powerful proof of the principle we are discussing. Great results in human life are never accomplished without great forces. The change of a world's convictions, the renewal of its religious thought, the readjustment of the lines of its religious allegiance, have not been accomplished without the expenditure of immense personal force, the application of the largest resources of energy and strength in character. There must have been unbounded courage to undertake the task, and even dream of the conversion of a world in which there were not as yet five hundred believers. The continuation of the labor through years and decades and centuries bears witness to the unflinching persistence of those who carried it on. The triumphs of the Church have cost unspeakable effort, inestimable sacrifices; and effort and sacrifice only come out of the strongest natures. And so we have

The Missionaries.   151

only to point to the map of the world's religious states, and compare it with one which might have been drawn a hundred years before Christ, to summon a witness to the presence of the most indomitable vigor in Christian souls all through the Christian ages.

As we seek the records once more, we find that the spirit which has founded these missions and which has already overcome one third of the population of the globe began with the beginnings of Christianity. It dates from the day in which Jesus called his disciples together and sent them forth to "all the world," to preach the gospel. All the apostles had this spirit. It was the motive of their work. It is the spirit which ever since has marked the administration of the affairs of Christendom with aggressive zeal and the energy of a conviction which burns for converts. From the beginning, one characteristic of Christianity which has never failed nor varied in any age or clime has been its unflagging aim to push its borders and spread its influence as fast and as far as human power could carry them.

First of all the great missionaries, the

worthy leader of an illustrious band, was Paul. He was the earliest to catch the thought of Christ that the gospel was for all men, and that by its very terms the exclusiveness of Judaism was abolished forever. To him we owe the christianizing of Europe, and he took all Europe into the field of his labors. He traversed the continent from the hills of Syria to the coasts of Spain, touching all the great cities and laying in them the foundations of the great world-church of the future. To him we owe the capture of the great centres from which the Christianity of the Empire pushed out its lines of influence. Rome, Corinth, Ephesus, Thessalonica, all held churches which felt his fostering care and received his anxious thought. In them were established the first mission-stations of the gospel, and in them Paul met the opposition and the contempt of Jew and Gentile, as he unfolded to cold and unsympathizing hearts the glad tidings of the new comer into the world's life.

There is no finer spectacle in history than that of the great leader of Christian missionaries sallying forth in poverty and in obscurity, a stranger in a great world, with no friend but his God, with no warrant of safety or of success save in the cause for which he went and the courage which filled his heart, meeting indifference with zeal, persecutions with patience, opposition with firmness, and discouragement with a deeper faith. There certainly never was a harder test of zeal, of enterprise, of courage, of endurance, of persevering activity than this man, single-handed against the world, unsustained even by the Christians whom he represented, turning to the gentile world, which showed not one friendly face, and starting on his work of conversion. Worldly wisdom would not have predicted much from that expedition when Paul set sail for Cyprus on his first journey. Still less would it have looked for anything more from him, when in later years it saw him chained to a soldier's wrist, in the streets of Rome, or when he bowed his head to the executioner's sword. Little indeed was there in these events to hint that his would yet be, next to that of Jesus Christ, the most famous name in all history; and yet to-day, in the heart of the most populous and famous of all modern cities, there rises a splendid dome, the work of London's great architect, to carry to all the world the fame of Paul the Apostle, the captain of the missionaries of Jesus Christ.

From Saint Paul onward the missionary spirit never flagged nor failed in all the Church. Its representatives appear in every age. Heart seemed to catch it from heart, and from age to age the work was handed on. In olden times, when the tidings of invasion were to be spread through the wild and sparsely settled country-side, or the levies summoned for attack, the fires were kindled on the hill-tops, beacons flashed from peak to peak, as if one flame kindled another. So from age to age, from church to church, from heart to heart, flashed the fires of missionary enterprise in the Church, rousing the loyal and stirring the faint heart with the marvellous enterprise of the seeker after souls.

Gibbon says, "The progress of Christianity has been marked by two glorious and decisive victories, one over the learned and luxurious Romans, the other over the warlike barbarians of Scythia and Germany." Foremost of these tribes, the sturdy and aggressive conquerors of Rome, were the Goths; and in proportion as they appeared pre-eminent among their fellows, did they excite the ambition of Christian hearts to conquer them for the cross. And when in the dispersion of the Christians by Gallienus, numbers of them were distributed in Gothic communities, the captives would not be silenced, but pressed the claims of their faith upon the nation with which they were domiciled, until many a convert rewarded their faithful zeal, and the foundation was laid for the Christianity of Middle Europe. And Ulphilas, himself a Goth and afterward a bishop, gave his life to the spreading and up-building of the faith. It was he who with infinite pains invented an alphabet for his people and then translated for them the whole of the Bible, save, it is said, the books of Chronicles and Kings, which he deemed too full of the stories of war for his turbulent people. And thus through the courageous enterprise of this man, the first of those translations was made, which have finally put the Bible into the native tongue of almost every nation and people upon the face of the globe and given the missionaries their mightiest weapon in the moral renewal of the world. For everywhere the men who go to win the souls of the heathen carry with them, as the source of their power and the authority by which they speak, this sacred volume. And wherever they bring it and place it before mankind, it wins its way, past criticism, past prejudice, past hostility, down to the reason and the conscience of mankind.

The time would fail to tell in detail of all the brave souls who entered into the missionary work in the early centuries. In the fifth century Saint Patrick wrought his ever-famous work in Ireland. John Richard Green has said that "when the Scotch-Irish Christianity burst upon western Christendom, it brought with it an enthusiasm, an energy, an earnestness greater than any it found there." In the sixth century Saint Columba begun a holy work amid the scenes which Black's pen has made so famous in the West Highlands of old Scotia, —

"When Christian piety's soul-cheering spark,
 Kindled from heaven between the light and dark
 Of time, shone like the morning star."

In the seventh century there occurred an incident in the streets of Rome of special interest to all who reckon their pedigree from English stock. Passing one day by a slave-market, a young deacon in the Church noted the white bodies, the fair faces, and the golden hair of some youths who were exposed there for sale. "From what country do these captives come?" he asked of the traders who brought them. "They are English,—Angles," was the answer. "Not Angles," was the answer of the young deacon, "but angels." Years passed on and the youth became pope under title of Gregory the Great. But he had never forgotten the fair-haired slaves nor their land, and he sought an opening to send them a missionary who should convert them to Christ. It was a Roman abbot, Augustine by name, who was selected. He and his followers entered the island from the very spot where a century before Hengist the Englishman had first landed on the Isle of Thanet. The monk came on a different errand from that which drew the bold warriors from Jutland, but his too was a mission of conquest and one which in the end cost no less of strength, of sacrifice, of courage than the long wars which reduced England to civilization. Side by side with the men who gave England political form, freedom, law, and constitutional government struggled and strove the men of God who established the power of Christianity in the realm, and so did their share toward promoting the land to the eminence she holds among nations.

But now, with the days of the Reformation, with Europe substantially Christian, the missionary spirit sought new worlds in which to spend its powers and bestow its zeal. And these came to hand, for new realms had been opened by the discovery of the Cape of Good Hope and the new route to the Indies; while Columbus had just laid the new world of the west a gift at the feet of Europe. With these new realms came a spirit which sought to conquer and to convert them. As the world expanded before them, Christians seemed to hear the words of Christ sounding with new emphasis in their ears, "Go ye into all the world and preach the Gospel to every creature." With the new call they girded themselves for fresh toils.

And here we meet the name of that consecrated soul who was the pioneer of eastern missions, Saint Francis Xavier. It may be truthfully said that Martin Luther gave him to the world; for when Luther reformed the Protestant branch of the Church, the power of his influence reacted upon Rome, and caused a season of repentance and purification to prevail there. The sturdy old friar purified the life of Mother Church at the same time that he created Protestantism; and foremost among the instrumentalities for effecting that renewal was the Society of Jesus, whose famous founder was Ignatius Loyola. This soldier-priest took under his especial care the careless, pleasure-loving, brilliant scion of the house of Xavier, till he made him his convert and won his whole soul to the work of the cross. And when John III. of Portugal desired to send some one who should plant Christianity in India, Xavier embraced with joy the perilous and awful undertaking. Penniless and solitary, he embarked upon a strange vessel for the port of Goa. Here in the midst of depravities which shocked and repelled him, he worked with unflagging zeal to reform and to convert. He was insensible to danger and shrunk from no privation and no pain; from town to town he strove single-handed to make a home for the true faith in the hearts of these heathen. With unswerving courage he faced alike the rage of the idol-priests, the perils of the pestilence, and the dangers of the earthquake. He loved his work, and took all its privations and its sufferings with a patient and a manly heart. Moved at last to go and plant the gospel in China, he had hardly landed upon that hostile coast when he was called from his work. There on the dreary beach, in the wasting agonies of a fever, he died with the words on his lips, "In Thee, O Lord, have I trusted, let me never be put to confusion." Thus died, like Moses before the promised land, a devoted missionary of Jesus Christ; and let no Protestant fail to remember that long years before a missionary from the Church of the Reformation had ever set foot in the East, this courageous man had pushed forward with the cross, the forerunner of that great host that has since encamped about Asia, till its ancient

The Missionaries. 161

kingdoms of error are beleaguered by the armies of the true God and his Christ.

The missionary spirit seemed to fit with especial aptness the minds of the Jesuits. Their fanatical zeal, their magnificent discipline, their austere life, all qualified them for this work which took them from all the things they most loved to the ends of a wild and savage earth. They early found their way in large numbers to South America. There they obtained a strong foothold and wrought a good work in rescuing the mild and peaceful natives from the cruelties of Spanish slavery and establishing them in orderly communities. And all through North America, from the St. Lawrence to the Gulf of Mexico, we find traces of the work of these brave men, lay brothers and priests, who labored with a dying race to give them the gospel, to redeem them from their evil lives, and at last to snatch them from the pains of purgatory. I know that the Jesuit's name has become synonymous with craft and selfish arts in religion. I am thankful beyond expression that the mission of these men in this wilderness was a failure, and that the wild and savage Iroquois frustrated all their plans. For thus was the day helped on which gave America to freedom and a pure Gospel. But for their heroic endurance, their daring, and their enterprise let us give all honor to these men; and if any one questions whether Christian faith is favorable to firmness of fibre in character and courage in action, let him read the recital of the Jesuits in North America. He will never repeat the query.

But up to the beginning of the present century, the Protestant churches had little of the missionary spirit. Indeed it would scarcely be believed in circles so committed to the missionary work as our evangelical churches are to-day, that a hundred years ago the practical temper of these same churches was absolutely opposed to missions to the heathen. It is less than a century since a young man pleading in a British assembly of churches for missionary work among the heathen was silenced by the venerable chairman, who exclaimed, "Sit down, young man; when the Almighty wishes to convert the heathen he will do it without your help or mine." In 1810, Adoniram Judson and four others inquired of the General Association of Independent Ministers, meeting at Bradford, Massachusetts, whether they might expect support from a missionary society in this country or must commit themselves to foreign help; and in the face of strong adverse public sentiment, the American Board was formed that same year. That spirit passed away long years ago, and since those days a steady column of workers has been moving to heathen lands to carry the good tidings of joy to all people.

The list is a long and honorable one. It includes such men as William Carey, the poor shoemaker who founded the Baptist Missions in India, and Henry Martyn, the thoughtful and educated Cambridge graduate who gave up his life in the work of Asiatic missions, and Reginald Heber, whose two years in India immortalized him, though it took his life first. The world is the brighter and better for such lives. Does it seem as if the career of John Coleridge Patterson could have been more useful if he had buried himself in his studies at Oxford, or that David Livingstone could have bestowed his life to any better advantage by staying at home and vegetating in England than he did by those brave years in which he labored to open the way for missionary effort in the very heart of Africa, and to "heal the open sore of the world," the negro slave-trade?

The world does not yet begin to know what it owes to these men and women, who have given their lives to the introduction of Christianity into foreign lands. Their work ripens but slowly, but it ripens all the same. These lands lie in wintry sluggishness now, but sometime we shall be surprised at the start they will give into Christian life. Meantime how fine the work, how manly and how brave, which these heroic souls are bestowing! It is like the toils and sacrifices of our Puritan fathers on old Massachusetts Bay. For they were striving to plant a commonwealth of God upon the rugged coasts of the New World; while the Christian missionaries are seeking to plant that city of God in every land on earth.

VII.

THE PHILANTHROPISTS.

There is a greater army
That besets us round with strife,
A starving numberless army,
At all the gates of life.
                    LONGFELLOW.

Who the Creator loves, created might
    Dreads not.
                    COLERIDGE.

Any man who puts his life in peril in a cause which is esteemed becomes the darling of all men. — EMERSON.

Before the eye of a purified reverence neither the giants of force nor the recluses of saintly austerity stand on so high a pedestal as the devoted benefactors of mankind. The heroes of honor are great; but the heroes of service are greater. — MARTINEAU.

VII.

THE PHILANTHROPISTS.

IN the heart of the Eternal City stood a building which may fairly be called typical of the ancient civilization. The Coliseum, vast and gray, with its tiers of seats encircling that arena which was the focus for so many thousand eyes, was a natural outgrowth of the society which fell with it. It was the theatre where brute courage was put on exhibition to furnish a sensation for a brutal curiosity. It was the scene where applause was quick to reward the strong arm, the stubborn will, the stolid nerves which would not flinch at pain. It was the sign of deep degeneracy and moral degradation. For when men are so at a loss for pleasures that they seek them in the spectacle furnished by the sacrifice of their own highest ideals; when they prostitute the courage they honor to the entertainment of a holiday rabble; when they debase the manly vigor which has won their national eminence into a show for jaded voluptuaries, then surely their shame is almost complete. But even in the moral darkness of such an environment, one bright ray gleams. It is the fact that even in this riot of bad passions, the old reverence for personal force still asserts itself.

There is hardly a city in modern Christendom which will not show an edifice equally characteristic of contemporary ideals. In every Christian community you may find some hospital or some asylum, some reformatory for evil natures or some shelter for diseased bodies, some building which bears witness to the universal Christian sentiment of helpfulness and regard for the weak. No matter which of this class is chosen, it will be a typical Christian edifice. It will stand for sentiments, moral forces, social convictions, as remote as possible from those which reared the Coliseum. But in one particular it will symbolize the same things. It will be a monument to a courage as real, a manliness as vigorous, a fortitude as unflinching, as ever prolonged the excitements of a Roman holiday.

Lest this seem a forced or an extravagant claim, consider its grounds in the facts of our civilized and christianized life.

The impulse to philanthropy comes no doubt from a susceptible heart or a quickened moral nature; and the moral awakening of mankind at the appeal of Christianity was the signal for all those activities to appear which have so alleviated and elevated human life. It has been a new world since Calvary and the Mount of Ascension. But the new spirit did not quench the old virtues; it only breathed upon them to make them glow more deeply. It did not dry up the sources of the active and aggressive spirit; it only opened new channels in which it might run. The philanthropic passion, the zeal for humanity which Jesus Christ awakened in man, may move him to new undertakings on his brother's behalf. But to carry on these works calls for the same qualities of courage, fortitude, and persistence, the same disregard of personal danger, the same tenacious hold on a difficult purpose, as have ever been the price of great accomplishments. The seed of philanthropy may be in a man, but it will never become a fruitful tree without courage, strength, and aggressive force. Many a man would like to help his fellows, if he only had the personal force; but there is no single detail of practical helpfulness to mankind which does not make large demands upon the strongest natures. You may sympathize with suffering men and women and long to relieve their physical pains. But have you the courage to hasten with the surgeon when he seizes his splints and bandages and goes to some railway wreck? Or could you pack your bag and go with the Red Cross nurses to the city devastated by the yellow fever or the cholera? You have faith in the latent spark of good in every man and would like to put your faith at work. But could you face a prison full of felons, mad with desperate hate, and without a weapon or a blow teach them the necessary lesson of submission to the authority of will? Or could you toil day after day among these same moral outcasts with only the courage of hope to strengthen you in your efforts to reclaim them? You love the practices of temperance and of purity, and want to see them the custom of mankind. But can you plant yourself in your personal practice where you would like all men to stand, and then, impervious to hostility, indifference, scorn, satire, resistance, slander, press the good you represent upon the unwilling minds of your fellow-men? It is a long way from the philanthropic impulse to its establishment in life. To feel the one demands only the gentle heart; to accomplish the other requires the stout will, the unflinching nerve, the aggressive resolve.

Perhaps there is no more striking illustration of how philanthropy, that enthusiasm for humanity which was born with Jesus Christ, though starting from a different impulse, comes to the same end and calls for the same spirit as the heroic temperament, than we may find in the Sanitary and the Christian Commissions during the Civil War in America. Here were two great organizations, thoroughly representative of the Christian character and civilization. They were the fruit of humane and Christian dispositions; they represented the charity, the sympathy, the tenderness of the American people, their trained conviction that the relief of suffering is a duty, and their almost unanimous belief that the moral welfare of a man is as important as his physical good; they embodied the noblest ideals of the Christian Church as these are set forth in the parable of the Good Samaritan. With an impulse so entirely Christian, it will not be questioned that these great auxiliary bodies were entirely typical of the spirit of Christ in human hearts after nineteen centuries of its prevalence on earth. But mark how identical was the response of this spirit to the call for courage, daring, and energy, with the behavior of the armies of the Union, the modern type of the primitive fighters of the world. It is written in the history of that struggle with what strength and persistence the work of the great Commissions was wrought, at what cost of personal effort, by what deeds of personal courage, with what energy and heroism. Wherever the soldiers went, there went the agent of the Commissions. When the battle began to rage, he was as prompt at the front as the troops themselves; he pressed to the field when the fire was hottest, to bring off the wounded; he went into the trenches and to the outposts on the picket line; he eased the pangs of the dying, gave Christian burial when possible, and marked the graves of the dead; and when all was done he sent to the far-off home the tidings which saved many a stricken heart from the terrible suspense which added such a heavy burden to bereavement; he cared for friend and for foe; he tended the sick, aided the returning prisoner, protected the helpless, sent the penniless on his way, and fed and clothed him as he went. And to do all this he shared the soldier's lot, endured the same privations, ran the same risks to liberty, limb, and life, and was to all intents and purpose his comrade in arms. The humane impulse of this noble band was wrought into deeds at the same cost of body and of heart as the patriotic impulse of the soldier. The love of mankind led to the same dangers, burdens, sufferings as the love of country. Nor did the philanthropic spirit, the most profound perhaps which ever glorified the horrors of war, abate one particle the heroic dispositions which it needed for its own incarnation in deeds.

Sometimes in the heat of war's contention the philanthropic instinct comes into direct collision with the coarser traits of the soldier. Then it acquits itself in no contemptible fashion, but so as to command the proud respect of all who love a bold and determined action. Such an incident comes to us out of that bitter war of 1870 between the French and Germans. General Ambert tells the story of a train of wounded Frenchmen who were marched for five hours from the field of battle, till they came at last to Janville. The poor sufferers were ready to drop with fatigue and with pain; but when they reached the public square a German officer ordered the convoy to keep on to Toury, a three hours' journey farther. "No, no," cried the wounded men, " leave us by the roadside. if you will; we cannot go farther." At this moment there appeared the superior of the hospice of Janville, Mother St. Henry. She confronted the officer. The woman of peace joined issue with the man of war. "Sir," she exclaimed, "these wounded men do not belong to you; they are my property. I will not have them dragged any farther." The officer resented her interference and would have sent the men on; but he could not bear down her commanding and authoritative will. "No more of this," she cried. "It is dastardly to make the wounded suffer needlessly. Driver, take out your horses." The convoy went no farther. The noble courage of the tender-hearted nun had vanquished the rough soldier.

These examples, it is true, may be alleged as only new fruits from the old root and branches of war. Take away its rough discipline, it is said, and you will lose the product also. But what shall be thought of those instances without number in which this same spirit has ripened from the mild training of peace? The courage of philanthropy, if we may coin a phrase, is in modern life an every day requirement. The great catastrophes of our times, the tragedies of the railway, the horrors of accident in the mines, the devastations of flood and tornado, are almost daily calling some detachment of the innumerable army of those who love their kind to scenes as dreadful as the battlefield. When the cholera or the yellow fever fills a community with the panic of fear, the fleeing people always leave behind them a determined band of men and women, fit exponents of the Christianity in whose spirit they have been trained, whose only thought is of their suffering fellows, and who are prepared to give life itself if need be, in the ministry of relief. Florence Nightingale, discharged from her voluntary service in the Crimea, becomes the pioneer in reforms and sanitary progress in the hospitals and homes of England. Clara Barton, closing her labors with the national armies when the last volunteer was mustered out, entered upon a work as useful and as heroic, in organizing and leading those large forces of philanthropy which wear the red cross of Geneva. The same women, or their daughters in the spirit, who fed the hungry soldier, changed his rags to comfort, nursed him in hospital, and gave their best strength to the care of all his needs and interests, — these women to-day are scattered up and down the land, doing the same work for these peaceful years as taxed the strength and courage in those war-days. They are struggling to stem the great tides of pauperism, idleness, and ignorance which have for years poured in upon America. They hold large responsibilities in the government of every

The Philanthropists. 177

hospital, charity board, and reformatory. They put protecting arms about little children, and stand between weak women and the tyrants and the villains who oppress or pursue them. They constitute an immense and indomitable army arrayed in a relentless struggle against the power of the saloon and the drink-habit.

The quarter-century of peace in America since the close of the Civil War has witnessed a great awakening of the moral powers of society against the evils of society. With a fuller sense than ever this world had before of the gravity of its sinfulness and corruption, Christian men and women have shown a larger courage than ever to meet and overcome social evils, a more resolute front, and a more aggressive advance. Ours is called a material age, a mercenary and a scientific age, and we are assured that the future will remember us as devoted to the physical life and its claims. But it is an open question whether the last half of the nineteenth century will not be renowned as much for its interest in the humanities as for its material progress. Through all the sordidness and secularity of the time there has run a broadening stream of humane energy and aggressive love for mankind. It may be doubted if there ever was an age which showed such a vast interest in man as man, labored so patiently for his advancement, or undertook so many humble and modest offices in his behalf. The world is teeming with organizations to relieve the unfortunate and to reform the bad. There is not a village large enough to support a church which does not maintain a benevolent society too; not a town is without its poor-house; vast hospitals here and there; schools and houses of reform for the criminal, asylums for the insane, homes for the orphan, the helpless, the incurable, the aged. And these are the evidences, outward and patent, of that positive vigorous philanthropy which marks the present day. It differs from the philanthropy of the past chiefly in its hopefulness and courage; it is a more sanguine charity; it approaches disease and physical foulness with a braver faith in the possibility of their removal; it deals with moral depravity in the spirit of the injunction to overcome evil with good. There is to-day no disease so malignant or so foul that it can deter humane hearts from ministering to its victims and resisting its ravages; there is no poverty so abject as to discourage the faithful disciples of the new charity; there are no felons so depraved as to daunt the fearless souls bent on errands of reform and reclamation. The ancient forms of courage which culminated in the clash of the armed onset could not bear comparison with this finer, firmer heroism, which shrinks at no moral or physical odds, but plants itself across the path of the pestilence or attacks the inert ignorance of a peasantry or a city lodging-house population, determined to exterminate the disease and to break up the mental sloth. It is easy to find the mere animal aggressiveness which has wielded most of the weapons in past ages and has pitted men against one another in physical combat. That is no rare trait; nor is it one which can any longer command the admiration once accorded to it. The call is now for the strength and the courage which can confront and attack "principalities and powers," grapple with the swarming dangers to the physical man which lurk in earth and air and water, or cope with the subtler and more formidable foes of the spiritual man which ambush in the perverse will, the depraved affections, the dull obstinacy, or the inflexible pride of evil natures.

No life in modern times exhibits this new type of courage and of strength in more impressive form than that of the man who almost created the latter-day meaning of the word "philanthropist." The career of John Howard was a long struggle with evils which afflicted the bodies and souls of the men and women of his generation. He was indeed an incarnation of Christian love. The motive of his life was the two great commandments. But he had a will of steel to do the bidding of that heart of love. His crusade against the enormities and abuses in the prisons of Great Britain put the severest strain upon the tenacity of his purpose and the courage of his faith. He found that numberless persons against whom the law had failed to prove any crime, or whom it had acquitted, were detained for months in foul prisons merely because they could not pay their jailers' fees. He undertook to overthrow this petty and demoralizing tyranny. He saw the direct way to a reform of this abuse, in the abolition of the whole system of fees and the payment of a salary to all prison officers. But that way was blocked by the giant which has checked so many reforms in England,—the inert bulk of old custom. Could he show a precedent for his demand? It required a personal visit of inspection to every prison in England to convince him that there was none. But then his courage rose to make the bold demand that humane Englishmen should make a precedent. The answer to that appeal was a law which ended this grave injustice and was the prelude to sweeping sanitary enactments.

But the whole condition of prison administration was disheartening to any lover of mankind. It might well have deterred a man less determined. To him it was only the occasion for more comprehensive plans and more thorough and exhausting labors. Let those who suspect the milder virtues of any softness or suppose that they begin and end in a yielding amiability, read anew the story of this man's self-appointed pilgrimage from nation to nation in Europe, seeking the dismal secrets of its prisons, breathing the noisome airs of its dungeons, consorting with criminals, paupers, the neglected, and the plague-stricken, that he might remove some of their miseries and ameliorate their condition. Let them picture him forcing his way into the breeding-places of the pestilence, where no companion dared follow him, even embarking in an infected ship that he might by experience learn all the horrors of the inhuman and inadequate quarantine of the time, pleading with the judgment of his contemporaries that his persistence might not be attributed to "rashness or enthusiasm, but to a serious and deliberate conviction," and dying at last from disease contracted in the labors he took upon himself in a noble emulation of his Master. The tales of the Crusaders may be scanned in vain to find aught that parallels this chivalrous tenderness, this indomitable patience, this heroic bravery. Well did this man merit the eulogy of Bentham! "In the scale of moral desert the labors of the legislator and the writer are as far below his as earth is below heaven. His kingdom is of a better world; he died a martyr after living an apostle."

It may be urged that such a life as Howard's was only possible in a society in which human sinfulness and ignorance had begotten pain and oppression, and that in that ideal state to which man is advancing, the very perfection of his conduct will remove at once the provocative to this humane energy and the conditions which keep it vigorous. But two probabilities may be suggested which rob this objection of its force. First, it is too much to expect that mankind will ever be freed, even in a perfected moral state, from

> "The heartache and the thousand ills
> That flesh is heir to."

Nature will see to that, in her rude violence and untamable excesses which no civilization can ever subdue. The winds, the waves, the rushing floods, the trembling earth, the lightning, and the snowstorm will be man's rough trainers in physical vigor and in the lower forms of courage. No earthly wisdom or strength will avert those accidents which test the coolest heads and the stoutest hearts. The coward will always be contemptible; the brave man will never lose his high rank. The indomitable resolution which carried Hannibal over the Alps; the contempt of death which led the Norsemen across stormy waters to hostile shores; the scorn of cowardice which glorified the slaughter-field of Balaclava; the heroism which made the sinking of the Cumberland more splendid than any victory, could all be shown in a warless world, where man had only to maintain the struggle against Nature, his own faith in the spiritual forces, and his mastery over himself. Secondly, due allowance must be made for the accumulation of moral energy which is continually going on in the human race. This is the process which is elevating the physical life of man, and generation by generation developing and perfecting his bodily powers, until it fits him for achievements impossible to the savage. It is the process, moreover, which is enlarging his knowledge, his command over mind and matter, his insight into the secrets of the universe, and his ability to use its most subtle and gigantic forces. Heredity, memory, the currents of a finer physical life in our veins, the spirit of a loftier thought in our minds, are forever deepening the channels and increasing the momentum of our progress, and diminishing the possibility of reversion to a lower grade of being. Must we not expect the same process to go on in the realm of the moral nature, strengthening every noble passion, and putting all that is worthy of perpetuation in the soul beyond the reach of decay or of disuse? If we may believe with Herbert Spencer that "the ultimate development of the ideal man is logically certain," we may surely trust that that fact includes the preservation of whatever is best out of his past. And until we are prepared to say that the force and the courage of the earlier manhood is a part of the legacy which ought to be rejected, we may trust in its perpetuation as a part of the equipment of the coming man, the human soul made perfect in Jesus Christ.

There is nothing, then, in the enlargement of the philanthropic spirit to make us fear that it will sap man's heroic nature and drain it of its energies. The philanthropists add their quota to the roll of heroes under the Christian spirit. The soft touch of love is still but the last refinement of courage and of strength. As long as the world lasts —

"True hearts will leap up at the trumpet of God,
  And those who can suffer can dare.
  Each old age of gold was an iron age too,
  And the weakest of saints may find stern work to do,
    In the day of the Lord at hand!"

VIII.

THE STATESMEN.

> YET remember all
> He spoke among you, and the man who spoke;
> Who never sold the truth to save the hour
> Nor paltered with Eternal God for power.
> TENNYSON.

> Nature, they say, doth dote,
> And cannot make a man
> Save on some worn-out plan
> Repeating us by rote.
> For him her old-world moulds aside she threw,
> And choosing sweet clay from the breast
> Of the unexhausted West,
> With stuff untainted shaped a hero new,
> Wise, steadfast in the strength of God, and true.
> LOWELL: on *Abraham Lincoln*.

The goal of history is in the fulfilment of the highest political ideal. It is the holy city; it is the new Jerusalem, the end of the toil and conflict of humanity.
MULFORD.

VIII.

THE STATESMEN.

THE highest practical work of the human mind is the organization of the State. It involves the profoundest thought and the most strenuous effort of which men are capable. A nation is the culmination of man's individual and social life. It is more than the assembling of men within certain lines of law; it is more than the forging of a compact between citizens; it is more than a society for the promotion of trade or manufacture. It is the embodiment of the spirit and the laws of human life in statutes and institutions; it is the organic growth, under human care and direction, of an extended political life; it is therefore the greatest organism which human thought and energy can produce. Thus it becomes the last and crowning manifestation in outward form of the thoughts, the convictions, the principles, and the spirit of a people.

This truth at once sets forth the work of the statesman in its proper dignity and scope. It is a labor which properly belongs to the very highest minds; it calls for the widest information and the broadest candor; it demands intense sympathy with the spirit of institutions and the genius of peoples. The statesman is more than a man who can manipulate social and political forces to the advantage of his nation. He is one who guides the currents of national life into the channels he builds out of institutions and laws, so that they go to swell the volume and the power of the world's life. He is endowed with the genius to see how the forces at work in his own age can be so directed and handled as to advance the interest of every human being. He need not be conscious always of the full meaning of his work; he may not see or foresee its relations to man's political progress or his growth in civilization. But the true statesman is he to whom God has given a supreme instinct, a divinely guided judgment, which leads him to do that one thing which is the best for his own nation and the best for all nations. He is the man who can discern the things which are essential, pre-eminent, absolutely needful to be done, and then bend strong energies to the achievement of them. His judgment singles out those stars in the heavens and those signs in the sea which guide man on the courses of God's providence, across the deeps of the long centuries, toward the haven of all nations and peoples.

This, therefore, is a type of human character in which these studies may fitly culminate. The statesman may be expected in every age of the world's history; his work will always be demanded. It is not limited to the period of human error and sinfulness. Its field is not restricted to the era of wars and rivalries, of selfish competitions and mutual fears. There will still be a necessity for it when the golden age has come and the nations learn war no more. Martyr and defender of the faith, hermit, monk, prelate, and knight are all ephemeral types, — the outgrowth of transient conditions of human society. The reformer's work will end with the millennial reign of righteousness, and the missionary will have no call when all men know the Lord; but the statesman, the organizer of social forces, the pilot of great States, the architect of institutions, the builder of codes, statutes, constitutions, — he is a perennial type, necessary in any age, a figure destined to perpetual eminence. We may conceive of his existence even in that "society of perfect beings" which Renan conceives would be so feeble a brotherhood. He would still find a career in blazing the path of progress and in conducting the columns of the advancing people along the ever new way. A State of some sort, an outward organism embodying his political and social ideals, man must always have; and the statesman must always be forthcoming to arrange the external life of the world in harmony with its principles and its ideals. It is pertinent, then, to ask whether in his present status there has been any falling away from the virility and force which have been his leading traits in all past ages; whether the Christian spirit in tempering his nature and raising his ideals has abated his energy or reduced his personal vigor; whether his latest achievements disclose a dwindling manhood or foretell a day when he will exchange courage for amiability and persistence for passivity; or whether we may still expect him, when the world has grown old in righteousness and ripe in the wisdom of the truth, to be the equal of the Cæsars and the Charlemagnes, the Hamiltons and the Lincolns of earth's earlier days, — in Emerson's words, "with strength still equal to the time; still wise to entertain and swift to execute the policy which the mind and heart of mankind require."

There are three particulars in which the statesman is called upon to exercise a strenuous courage and an inflexible purpose. He must be strong enough to have unwavering convictions; he must be brave enough to disregard the clamor of ignorance and of misapprehension; and he must have a persistent faith which will carry him over every obstacle between him and the goal of his purpose. These are the indispensable traits of the mind which organizes great ideas into national life. They will fit the millennium as well as they serve the present day.

The power to perceive the trend of the active forces of an age and foresee their results is a rare gift. Yet it is less rare than the courage to stand unfalteringly by one's convictions when they are formed. Ten men will see the truth of a principle for one who will avow and abide by the consequences of his conviction. There is a timidity of custom, a cowardice in the face of a change of belief, which holds the vast majority of men in thrall. How vastly is the power of that fear enhanced when fidelity to that conviction may destroy the settled calm of established institutions, break in upon a hundred vested interests, or plunge a great people into the calamities of war! Yet in this consists the very primary virtue of the statesman. He must follow the lead of his perceptions, at whatever cost to personal comfort or the temporary tranquillity of others. Cæsar at the Rubicon, taking all the hazards of that hidden way which led him to the imperial throne and Rome to the mastery of the world, will always be the type of the statesman, with the instinct to perceive and the courage to take the only way by which the world can go on to its grander life. The early colonists of America, putting aside their old-world traditions and applying to their own communities new principles and practices, displayed the courage of the largest statesmanship. The framers of the Declaration of Independence likewise evinced at once the strongest sense of the inevitable course of events and the stoutest courage of their convictions, when they declared the united colonies to be "free and independent States," affirming that "they are absolved from all allegiance to the British crown and that all political connection between them and the State of Great Britain is, and ought to be, totally dissolved." It was no idle promise to pledge to the support of this act their lives, their fortunes, and their sacred honor. That vow was tested by the seven long years of peril, hardship, sacrifice, and death which forever decided the new direction in which the world's political development should proceed. But only in this same way, by unflinching faith in great truths which have become clear to the mind and in the brave espousal of them without regard to consequences, can statesmanship ever secure its great end,— the elevation of man in the development of human institutions.

So too the statesman must disregard

the clamor of ignorance and of misapprehension which opposes every advance in thought or the founding of institutions. The moral and intellectual inertia of man, even in his best estate and when he is most sincere and devoted to truth and right, makes the task of a wise statesmanship a test of heroic tenacity. Men will reject the most undoubted good when it comes in a novel guise or involves the trying changes of reform. John Fiske has well called the transition from the colonial to the constitutional government in America "the critical period of American history." It required years of debate and persistent agitation under the courageous leadership of Washington, Hamilton, and Madison to convert the American people to that theory of organization and government which has made our experiment so signal a success. Nor was the deliverance of the nation from the destructive element of internal slavery secured at any less price of brave effort, persistently made in the teeth of popular resistance.

The third heroic trait in the statesman is the power of sustained perseverance in overcoming the natural obstacles and difficulties which must hinder the wisest policy and delay the most desirable changes. This, of course, is the test of all moral strength, which becomes conspicuous in the statesman because of the grand scale upon which his work is necessarily done and the strong light of publicity which shines upon him. When the elder Pitt said that he and he only could save England out of the perils she was in, there lay between him and his success the personal dislike of the King, a hostile majority in Parliament, and the armies and fleets of France. To overcome such obstacles, the common lot of all great statesmen, and to turn his very difficulties into splendid triumphs was a heavy tax upon even that indomitable spirit. So, too, the great Richelieu, bending all his genius toward effecting the unity of France, must overcome, in the attainment of his purpose, the unfriendliness of the Pope, an embittered queen, conspiring nobles, valiant Huguenots, the malice of Spain and of Italy. Over such impediments must these great guides of political destiny clamber, to attain the consummation of their far-reaching purposes. And the feat is no less a one for the will and the moral nature than it is for the intellect. Time, civilization, Christianity, the millennial era itself, will abate none of these qualifications for the statesman, — the courage to believe, to resist pressure, and to overcome obstacles.

The advance of Christian ideas and the increasing sway of the Christian spirit have gradually developed and elevated the character of statesmanship. More and more its exercise has been in the behalf of righteousness and the pure ideals of the gospel. The brotherhood of man gains increasing recognition with every revision of national codes and constitutions. Larger provision is made for peace and amity between the nations; justice and righteousness are receiving more than a nominal respect. Thus the work of the statesman grows more closely allied to the labors of the Church and its agents. For in the proportion in which the State incorporates Christian principles into her organism, in that same proportion must those who guide her policy become the agents of the kingdom of heaven. It becomes therefore an interesting question whether, in the most enlightened nations of these latest Christian centuries, any examples have been given of what we may expect from a Christian statesman, and whether the men of this type who in their labors have shown the most sympathy with Christian ideals have shown any decadence in manly force. To answer this question we may profitably cite two signal examples from among the leaders in the statesmanship of the nineteenth century, — Lincoln and Gladstone.

If we were seeking for a case of a public man dominated by the broad and fundamental principles of the Christian religion, a man whom no sect could claim, who nevertheless was deeply imbued with the essential spirit of the gospel, we might well rest our search at the name of Abraham Lincoln. He was a typical leader of men. He was the most conspicuous figure in a most critical period of national and international history; he was in the deepest sense of the word a religious man and a Christian man; he carried through all the trials of his four years of responsibility, anxiety, and sacrifice an unswerving faith in the guidance of God and a steadfast perception of the duty he owed to the Divine law. He was a man to whom the moral aspect of the great struggle always was foremost; nor could he ever, in any question of policy or of administration, divest himself of the sense of obligation to justice, righteousness, and love. He may unhesitatingly be taken as a type of the Christian statesman striving to embody in the policy of a desperate hour fidelity to the highest law, the Divine will and commandment. How well he sustains the standards we have set up, a glance at his work will show.

It was the mission of Abraham Lincoln to conserve the work of many centuries and many devoted heroes in the long struggle of mankind toward an era of universal peace. The war which preserved the Union did much more than that; it preserved the work of ages. The American Union is the culmination of a long series of political changes, away from that primeval condition of human society when there was in fact no society, but every man was for himself and against all his neighbors. Little by little, in the lapse of ages, larger and larger groups of men allied themselves for the sake of peace and security, that they might hold the turbulent in check while the necessary pursuits of life were followed. Family, clan, nation, — these were the successive steps by which men enlarged the scope of their alliances and compacts; and with each step the tranquillity of the world increased, and a larger share of human life was spent in peace and its pursuits. At length the wisdom of the American people, embodied in the genius of Hamilton and Madison, framed the Constitution, and advanced the human race one step further, by showing how separate States with all their own internal interests untouched could dwell in peaceful alliance. This was the solution of the last great problem in the quest for methods of peace and law among men. For it is evidence incontestable, framed in a great State instrument and displayed in the continuous life of an entire nation, that States, like individuals, can decide their differences not by brutal war but by systematic legislation or a common tribunal. The American Union is the highest political embodiment of Christianity; it is the highest proof of the possibility of a universal peace; it is the most convincing test of man's capacity for unity in diversity and diversity in unity. In this respect, this Union is the consummation of all the struggles of all men toward a state of universal peace. It is the hope and aspiration of mankind organized at length into a mighty nation.

No less a work than this was put in peril by the Rebellion. A tremendous test was applied to this great experiment in government and in political life. Setting aside all involved and secondary issues, the one great question decided in that struggle was whether this peaceful compact should be maintained, — a light to the nations and a perennial force for their improvement, — or whether its broken fragments should impede the progress of the whole human race. In the decision of that fateful question there was no more potent factor than the mind and will of Abraham Lincoln. He grasped the issue with unerring perception; with inflexible tenacity he persisted in the only course which could decide it aright. He kept before himself and he kept before the nation the one aim in which he and they must unite,— the preservation of the Union. The great principle that individual States may exist in pacific federation must be maintained at any hazard. Abraham Lincoln felt the meaning of the crisis which had come to America better than almost any other man of his time. He had the instinct of the highest statesmanship; he saw the one thing which was essential, pre-eminent, necessary. He had those moral qualities which we have decided are also to be looked for in the true statesman, — faith in his own conviction; imperviousness to the outcry of less clear-sighted men, their distracting persuasions, their irritation, or their hate; and a heroism almost without parallel in his patient and faithful adherence to this purpose through the four weary years of that exhausting struggle. Rarely has this world witnessed a sublimer spectacle than this simple, god-fearing man, holding fast to his one purpose of preserving the Union and moving unwaveringly on, through reverses and disappointments, harassed by treachery and indifference in camp and in counsel; harried by treason in the rear while he grappled with rebellion in the front; defied by foes, and mistrusted by friends; true to his conviction, unmoved by opposition, undismayed by difficulties, until his wonderful task was done, and he had made secure the work which had cost the struggle and the sacrifice of the ages. All the adamantine firmness of the man is revealed in the words he uttered after four years of struggle and sacrifice, which discover a strength and a persistence as lasting as any trials it might be called to endure: "Fondly do we hope, fervently do we pray, that this mighty scourge of war may pass speedily away. Yet if God wills that it continue until all the wealth piled by the bondman's two hundred and fifty years of unrequited toil shall be sunk, and until every drop of blood drawn by the lash shall be paid by another drawn by the sword, as was said three thousand years ago so still it must be said, that the judgments of the Lord are true and righteous altogether." The statesman who could speak in such wise as that had lost none of the strength of manhood. His Christian spirit had engendered no feebleness of will; he was as wise as he was honest, as courageous as he was wise, and as strong as he was courageous. There need be no misgivings about the millennium if such natures shall multiply.

We find an equally impressive illustration of this vigorous spontaneity and freshness of manly spirit in the magnificent contest which for the last few years England's veteran statesman has kept up, in behalf of justice and a durable political arrangement between England and Ireland. There are many features of that battle which must extort a new admiration for the capacities of human nature from the most reluctant minds. The intellectual force of Mr. Gladstone would of itself entitle him to the highest distinction. His moral energy ranks him among the foremost men of the Christian era. That a man of fourscore years — long past the age at which most men retire from the mere labor of thinking and still further past the time at which the vast majority excuse themselves from adopting new theories or sympathizing with new plans — should advance beyond all the limits of his previous statesmanship and place himself at the head of his nation, in a severe and almost revolutionary crisis, is a noble demonstration of a whole and vigorous intellect. But that a political leader, nearing the close of his career, should be willing to peril his name, his power, and his popularity by espousing a measure certain to be received by his countrymen with hostility, and perhaps rejected with bitterness, gives one a new faith that political disinterestedness is not an utterly unknown quantity. Yet Gladstone crowns his remarkable traits with an invincible faith, — all the more striking as it stands in such marked contrast with the mood of his countrymen, — that human nature is the same in Ireland as it is elsewhere, and that it will respond to justice, fair-dealing, and generosity by loyalty and good-faith. He has brought imperishable renown to himself by a firm resistance to all the malice of partisan opposition and all the sincere hostility of an alarmed conservatism and selfish interest. In the face of all the obstacles his enemies have put in his way, he has persisted in his opposition to the policy of coercion and of force untempered by the higher views of justice. He stands to-day, pre-eminent among his contemporaries in his embodiment of a manly trust in the inherent honesty of human hearts, in the conquering power of equity, and in a policy which will bear the most lasting fruits of peace and national stability. He will be assigned a historic place among those who have been most eminent exponents of Christian principles as applied to the problems of statecraft, and hence as a representative of the vast gains mankind has made in the spirit of the Christ. Measure Gladstone with Xerxes or Alaric, and one has some conception of the vast growth of human ideals toward the model of the Sermon on the Mount. In that same estimate may be seen the stability of the manly vigor which knows no decay, nay, which shows with an enhanced brilliancy after nearly twenty centuries of Christian tutelage.

And now we leave this story of Christian heroism, Christian character, Christian achievements. It has set forth but imperfectly the types which Christian life has fostered. But has it not shown the favor and the encouragement which the Christian spirit gives to the active virtues, and the perpetuity which it bestows upon them? The test of the centuries has proved the power of Christianity to beget a manliness and a force as firm and as vigorous as any born of the old paganisms. The new courage is as stout as the old; the new heroes rival their ancestors in character. The expectation with which we entered on these studies is justified. The same strong traits reappear with each succeeding age, varying only to rise in dignity and refinement. Martyrs and defenders of the faith; hermits and monks; prelates and knights; reformers and missionaries; philanthropists and statesmen, — all have the same stout heart as beat in the breast of the primeval heroes. There is no waste of this germinal force from generation to generation. The Christian heroes display the spirit which all ages admire; and in all the tenacity and force of the active virtues, in personal energy, in unflinching courage, in aggressiveness, resolution, daring, and persistence, they show a finer quality which rivals and outshines all the examples of the elder world.

> "They climbed the dizzy steep of heaven
> Through peril, toil, and pain.
> O God! to us may grace be given
> To follow in their train."

THE END.

www.ingramcontent.com/pod-product-compliance
Lightning Source LLC
Chambersburg PA
CBHW020902230426
43666CB00008B/1281